7DAY.

D0265948

RESPONSIVE
LISTENING
THEATER TRAINING FOR
CONTEMPORARY SPACES

International Perspectives on Norwegian Theatre Academy (NTA)
at Østfold University College

There are two kinds of theatre schools: Those founded to feed the existing institutions, with young people trained to fulfill the traditional aesthetics; and those raising questions about the future of theatre. Most schools belong to the first category; unfortunately only few, maybe just five in all of Europe, to the second. NTA is clearly one of them: a place for aesthetic experiments, perception-based research, and engaged, upcoming artists.

>—Dr. Philipp Schulte, *Institute for Applied Theater Studies, Giessen, Germany*

Norwegian Theatre Academy represents a fresh, undogmatic attitude and an inquisitive approach to an art field in growth and progress. Employing an interesting list of resourceful people from the practical field, their Norwegian and international artists only serve to complement the picture, making this education relevant far beyond the many walls of the school. NTA educates for the future by equipping the students with the tools necessary for a meaningful life on various stages, in sync with a market that is continuously evolving and changing. NTA enriches Norwegian stage arts.

>—Sven Åge Birkeland, *Artistic and Managing Director, Bergen International Theatre (BIT)*

I thoroughly enjoyed my engagement with the Academy acting students. They were focused and fully engaged in the psychophysical process work through which we explored Samuel Beckett's later, shorter texts. It was a pleasure to work with them.

>—Phillip Zarrilli, *Artistic Director, The Llanarth Group*

I have just watched a former NTA student come to New York City and easily integrate herself into a wide variety of working situations with established artists. She did this with an ease that takes years for other young artists to navigate. The training at NTA created a versatile, supple, problem solving, and confident international artist whose value is immediately perceived.

>—Sxip Shirey, *Composer and Performer*

Kelly and I worked at NTA for six weeks with a group of graduating students on their final performance. It was an experience unlike any other we'd had working with students. We were invited to challenge the NTA students and expand their idea of what theater could be, but instead, we ourselves got pushed in unexpected directions and beyond our own limitations. The students at NTA are brave, adventurous, and mature artists beyond their years. The piece we made with them became something we couldn't have imagined, and we are grateful for the opportunity. The other faculty and staff at the school don't know the word "no" and always tried to figure out how to make even the craziest idea happen. I really believe we learned more than we taught, and our time in Fredrikstad remains one of the highlights of our creative careers. The school is a hotbed of new ideas and a haven for experimentation. If given the opportunity, Kelly and I wouldn't hesitate to come back, because we know that we would grow and greatly benefit from the experience.

—Pavol Liška & Kelly Copper, *Nature Theatre of Oklahoma*

NTA is not just a school but a laboratory for theater professionals. The Academy creates a forum in which students work together with professionals to explore new directions in performance. It is hard to find a more ideal environment to work in.

—Robert Johanson, *Actor and Director*

I have been back to Fredrikstad every year since my first workshop in 2007 and working at NTA is always a pleasure. As a facilitator and mentor, I want to do my absolute best because the students are always curious and engaged. Actually, it feels more like working with a group of emerging professionals than a body of students. My experience of working with performance in the UK has been that in art schools they have great ideas but poor technique. On theatre courses they have good technique but no ideas. NTA somehow offers what I think of as an art school education to theatre students. They are encouraged and equipped to have both good technique and great ideas. The system of invited guest artists means that students are continually exposed to new ideas and a great variety of ways of working.

—Joshua Sofaer, *Artist*

The students at Norwegian Theater Academy are bright, conscious, and sophisticated in their sense of form. They learn how to research, to place their profession in relation to various perspectives of art and society, which shapes them into strong stage artists and theatre makers.

—Victoria Meirik, *Director*

When I first came to the Norwegian Theatre Academy, I thought that I was coming to a conventional Drama school. On my first visit I realized this was far from the truth. I had come to an inspiring and revolutionary school with a very new way of training actors. The Norwegian Theatre Academy gives the actors a real sense of the empowerment of the self and independence to create their own performances with scenographers, who are also trained at the Academy. They use and work with what they receive from invited teachers from all over the world to create their own performances. This creates very creative challenges both for the actors and the scenographers, and I feel this has far reaching creative implications on what direction the theatre might take in the 21st century. It is a real privilege and very creative for me to be invited to teach at the Norwegian Theatre Academy.

—Nadine George, *Voice Studio International*

NTA provides a stimulating learning and teaching environment for students to explore the most creative and productive range of arts practices. Its unique identity is shaped by the core team of leading professionals committed to collaboration and to artistic research. The range of visiting artists provides a challenging, exciting and diverse environment feeding directly into the contemporary nature of the NTA community. Students at NTA foster learning, are deeply bound to process, and in turn they are inventive, diligent, critical, and assertive.

—Dr. Claire Hind, *Associate Professor & Course Leader,*
MA Theatre and Performance, York St John University

Teaching at NTA is like stepping into an amazing laboratory, where you not only get to share what you know, you get to test and refine it and risk and discover, with students who are unique artists themselves, unafraid to dive in and explore the possibilities of what Theater is, can, and could be. All of this happens in an atmosphere with clear and dedicated leadership and support. It is a singular place, an environment where current and emerging theater artists can push the possibilities and move our field into new, exciting territory, creating work that speaks to the "now" and will influence the future.

—Dan Safer, *Director and Choreographer, Witness Relocation, NYC*

RESPONSIVE LISTENING

THEATER TRAINING FOR CONTEMPORARY SPACES

Edited by Camilla Eeg-Tverbakk
and Karmenlara Ely

Brooklyn Arts Press • New York

Responsive Listening:
Theater Training for Contemporary Spaces
Edited by Camilla Eeg-Tverbakk and Karmenlara Ely

© 2015 Brooklyn Arts Press

ISBN-13: 978-1-936767-36-6

Cover design by Adrian Friis. Interior design by Benjamin DuVall. North American reviews by Joe Pan & Sam Hall.

Published in the United States of America by:
Brooklyn Arts Press
154 N 9th St #1
Brooklyn, NY 11249
www.BrooklynArtsPress.com
info@BrooklynArtsPress.com

Produced with Norwegian Theatre Academy (NTA)
at Østfold University College.

Distributed to the trade by Small Press Distribution / SPD
www.spdbooks.org

Library of Congress Control Number: 2015930684

10 9 8 7 6 5 4 3 2 1
First Edition

Contents

11   Introduction
        Karmenlara Ely and Camilla Eeg-Tverbakk

15   Yielding to the Unknown: Actor Training
        as Intensification of the Senses
        Karmenlara Ely

34   On Scenography
        Serge von Arx

39   On *Playing* a Text
        Camilla Eeg-Tverbakk

54   Manifesto In Praxis: Calling
        for a (Re)considered Approach
        to Training the Performer's Voice
        Electa Behrens

70   Scenography and the Visual
        at Norwegian Theatre Academy
        Karen Kipphoff

89   Text as Sound and Music
        Øystein Elle

98   *Zooming In*: Reflections on My Education
        at Norwegian Theatre Academy
        Veronika Bökelmann

107   A Good Thing: A Graduate's Tale
        Ivar Furre Aam

        Contributors

RESPONSIVE LISTENING

THEATER TRAINING FOR CONTEMPORARY SPACES

Introduction

Karmenlara Ely and Camilla Eeg-Tverbakk

The Norwegian Theatre Academy (NTA) at Østfold University College has built its reputation by questioning conventional theater practices and challenging normative ideas on methods of acting and scenography within a theater education. For many years NTA has focused on research as a driving force of our BA educations in acting and scenography. This has led us to high levels of both student and teacher experimentation, drawing on methods from the various art fields in order to create an original interdisciplinary methodology that places education between the traditions of the skill-based conservatory and studio-based art scholarship. In 2015, NTA founded the first and only MA in Scenography in Scandinavia out of our commitment to deepen the connection between theory and practice. The acting program at NTA, as highlighted by this volume, educates actors as creative artists able to both interpret others' works while developing their own original art practice, ranging from theater to performance art to all genres in-between. Throughout the three-year BA program, our teaching targets the development of each student's particular talents and interests. Graduates refer to themselves as actors, "stage artists," performance artists, or simply artists, a reflection perhaps of our interdisciplinary approach and also the type of work our students create, which is manifold. Our scenographers, likewise, pursue a range of expression when creating a space for the street, stage, or for an exhibition. Their goal is not to "decorate a stage," but to manifest an architectural and sensory potential for unfolding events. Crossing between different media, these scenographers invent their own approaches to architecture and experience as fluid responses to a given situation. This involved approach influences acting practices by generating a live and present dialogue between bodies in space.

Located at Østfold University College, one hour south of the Norwegian capital Oslo, in the small town of Fredrikstad, NTA holds a peripheral place in relation to the center of theater in Norway. For many years, NTA held the role of the "alternative" acting program in the country, as compared to the National Academy of the Arts in Oslo, which for around forty years served as the only acting program in the country. NTA today represents the interdisciplinary and experimental branch of contemporary theater training. This placement in relation to mainstream academia has provided us with a certain amount of freedom to test out and develop various pedagogies without interference. Our students benefit greatly from the workshops led by a wide range of visiting international artists and pedagogues, experts in the field who continue to influence the school's working methods as a reflection of active art practices in educational development. Theater education at NTA aligns itself with a historical avant-garde lineage, drawing on century-old traditions rooted in an interdisciplinary art field that is more strongly connected with popular theater traditions than its well-known literary counterpart. Working in the twenty-first century, however, often implies beginning with a dramatic text—or any kind of text—as much as from a devised, sensory, physical, or visual point of departure.

Introduction

Since 2003, after rising from its beginnings as a school for object-related theater, NTA has placed itself at the cultural foreground of intense interdisciplinary approaches to contemporary stage art. The Academy is always researching what kinds of methodologies might best support and serve contemporary experimentation within performing practices on global stages. This journey has taken our research and practice from what has been labelled "physical theater," through work with dance- and conceptual theater, to more recent research drawing on socially engaged art practices, relational strategies, and musicality and compositional approaches to theater making. To this end, scenographers and actors work closely together in conceptualizing and evolving projects as part of a collaborative process. Today at NTA, the actor is not the center of the work, nor is the director or scenographer; it is the space between creative elements and audiences that is embraced. The emphasis has always been to teach students to observe and interact with the relationship between practice and theory, art, and society.

This publication is a reflection on the foundational aspects of the pedagogy evolving through both our faculty- and student-led research. We focus in this volume on aspects of the acting education in particular, but include brief perspectives from the scenography practice because the programs are so intrinsically connected. All practices at NTA begin in response to a space, celebrating scenography and acting as mutually dependent disciplines that shape and challenge each other critically. In this volume, the Artistic Director of Scenography, Serge von Arx, reflects on the nature of scenography as it informs his approach to the crucial shaping of a total education. Authors Electa

Responsive Listening

Behrens, Øystein Elle, Camilla Eeg-Tverbakk, and the Artistic Director of Acting, Karmenlara Ely, reflect on the acting program and its various training modules, which are based on intensifying sensory awareness, transposable musicality, and rhythm, each crucial aspects of ensemble and performance. Karen Kipphoff contributes a photo essay that documents examples of the meeting point between the two programs, and two alumni authors, Veronika Bökelmann and Ivar Furre Aam, speak about their time as NTA students.

Our on-going research and development training is a practical means of activating inspiration in students of contemporary theater, which also includes the study of such subjects as contemporary philosophy, critical theory, sound, and relationality. Our theoretical tendencies lean toward discourses on listening, presence, sound, sensory relations to material and things, and composition in space and time. Much of this work reflects a contemporary thinking around subjectivity, with an aim of finding new and sustainable ways to understand our selves and our relation to the world in which we live and create. Whether we are working with text, creating inventive dramaturgies, improvising, or composing physical actions and movement on stage, the ability to listen and pay attention to resonances are, ultimately, what we rely upon to establish multiple layers of meaning in our material; these are the keys to developing melodies, rhythms, tones of expression. We focus on introducing our students to a number of well-known methodologies, choosing not to rely on any one in particular, as a way to have the students engage all possible influences while constantly questioning both methodology and aesthetics, in the hope that they develop their own.

Yielding to the Unknown: Actor Training as Intensification of the Senses

Karmenlara Ely

A performer's unique skill is in the art of not just invention, but response. It is therefore also necessary for the actor to investigate the world at the most intimate level of sensory practice, to discover what action implies. Even in Hamlet's essential dilemma, it is not just enough to ask the question what it means to be, but what the implications of action are. Theatrical action is framed by the global stage, where drama and representation have material impact (i.e. the effects of racism, bullying, warfare) while using complex devices of media and spectacle. On today's stages we are confronted with the efficacy of live action, and the implications of face-to-face relation. We make this clunky thing called "Theater" in an age of glossy production, digital prosthesis, viral media. We are human bodies that age, decay, feel pain and joy, and experience many things. How do we reflect on and share the failure and delight of the experience of the human being through the theater, without pandering to audiences or relying on emotional pornography? It's not enough to train actors to be vessels for great authors or directors. Actors as creative agents must both listen to their complex surroundings in order to respond to them, and in turn help us, their audience, re-encounter the world.

Responsive Listening

As practitioners we are presented with a problem: how to make theater that invites dialogue and intimacy through critical images and dynamic, sensory, spatial relationships. We seek theater where the bodies of all participants, spectator and performer, are acknowledged in space, via the senses, as being fully present and not "always-already departed," somewhere else. We live in a time where we are double-booked, asked to be multiple, and late. How then do we meet our audiences as collaborators, and bring to them the feeling of being invited, embraced, implicated, responsible? Here and present, capable of shared dreaming?

Conventional twentieth century representational modes like method acting or psychodramatic storytelling (each relying on the idea of a "4th wall") sometimes allow the audience to become too comfortable, despite how well a somewhat fixed world has been masterfully created by the actors. Championing this standard, or any standard, by itself sets limitations for training a contemporary performer seeking continually relevant staging, especially those who want an active, critical audience. It is a demand of many contemporary artists to interrogate the work they make as they are making it, in its process, as they struggle with form and content. African-American artist Adrian Piper, for example, uses the phrase "indexical present"[1] to describe a phenomenon in her work that draws critical attention to the moment, forming a social-political consciousness.

---

1   In "Shaivistic Reverberations: Exchanges Between Adrian Piper and Adelaide Bannerman," Bannerman states that, "Piper's work has consistently examined the relationships between the individual and the illusions that constitute realities that structure and shape our experiences of this world. She has done this primarily through her concept of the 'indexical present' (i.e., self-scrutiny of behavior in the moment it occurs) and its function within her installations and performance-related works. Her intent is to mobilize the type of self-examination that can transform consciousness and evoke changes to how one perceives the world and other individuals" (Bannerman 27).

Yielding to the Unknown

But its relevance goes beyond the topic of insidious sexism and racism she raises with her piece, *My Calling Card*: an indexical present calls us to reflect on how we act as we are acting. It asks us to reserve a space for critique not after, but during, the scene. To wake up, even if just for a moment.

The most interesting contemporary actors today, utilizing various methods and approaches, are calling their own presence into question. Postmodern dramaturgies have long been playing with form, and asking the actor to reimagine the dialectic space between that which is "me" and "not me" in a text or character task. Performers are even working outside that very dialectic as a direct challenge to the idea of a knowable "me" altogether. When entering a training process we are inherently asking the question of "how to act," or how to reflect on acting. It may be that technique is not the answer to this question, but that the answer is a reflexive opening of the question itself and provides an approach. In research-based acting practices, we can question reality as well as explode it, in the hopes of opening up other platforms of experience. Audiences want to see the actor struggle artfully with the very situation of theater, as illustrated by the influential work of Nature Theater of Oklahoma. Actors want to tell different stories than what is inherited from the archive.

Tethered to the mechanics of modernism, "systems" for actor training still inform many institutional expectations for the stage: rules for how it's done and not done, limitations in scoring and embodying text. The contemporary performing artist in an institution meets an interesting challenge when training freely across a variety of approaches. She becomes an actor without a master, responsible for researching, choosing, and experimenting with performance strategies to meet the work at hand. This challenges one to treat each project and space as unique, working through the senses and one's humanity. The unanswered questions of how to act and how to reflect on acting demand a continual ear in relation to the moment.

Action

While aspects of a personal journey and a relationship with the self are important to any artistic process, training at Norwegian Theatre Academy does not center around the inner life of the actor as an ideal. How do we destabilize and problematize the idea of the actor, while also calling what we do actor training? The answer partly has to do with how we define or understand *action*. The actor is the one (of several or many) who sets things in motion, who makes things happen in social space. This motion carries with it the implication of responsibility, calling one to consciousness and conscientiousness. Hannah Arendt in *The Human Condition* describes the open and unpredictable nature of action as a consequence of human freedom: by acting, we are free to start processes and bring about new events, but no actor has the power to control the meaning or consequences of his or her deeds. Every act sets in motion an unlimited number of actions and reactions without end. As Arendt puts it: "The reason why we are never able to foretell with certainty the outcome and end of any action is simply that action has no end" (233). Theatrical action with reflective capacities calls upon not just consciousness of social problems or justice, but also theatrical materials, theatrical time, expenditure, and exchange. Suzanne Jaeger, in *Staging Philosophy*, writes, "Stage presence can be defined as an active configuring and reconfiguring of one's intentional grasp in response to an environment. It is to be aware of the uniqueness of a particular audience and of certain features of a theatrical event rather than performing a perfect repetition of a familiar and well-rehearsed pattern of behavior" (122). So it stands that stage presences, or the state of being "awake" and not en-tranced by the idea of one's own acting or an obsession with perfecting one's self in front of an audience, demands an actor be playful and open in his or her collaboration with the audience. Theater practice imagined with the actor as creator/responder creates vivid and dynamic structures for play, inviting others into our rich dream worlds and aiming at shared dreaming, co-creating (rather than dramatic situations meant to showcase the actor's brilliance).

So then what is the acting "self"? The concept may be more poetically understood as a volatile sensory resonance than as an object of knowledge or a thing to be trained. Jean-Luc Marion, in *The Erotic Phenomenon*, describes the self in a way we can compare with Arendt's notion of action, as one's ethical collaboration with the unknown. The self is experienced, he says, as arriving from "elsewhere," always in possibility and in suspension, rather than in given objects and known certainties (71). As an actor, I often experience myself as a crisis, without ground. What gives me agency, gives me selfhood, is the leap inherent in the action of giving over fully to the other (giving my time, my listening, my expressions, my desire). In this way, writes Marion, I am put "on stage," through my surrender to the inevitable failure to know what will happen in advance. Surrendering to the spiral of ephemeral process actually helps me emerge. Being the first to love, for example, is an action, a subjectivity, that, from a state of poverty and belief, allows the other to appear. It is generous. You could say one engages the self by the throwing of oneself fully into the possibilities of a space, which answers the call of a space while providing the creation of another call. The self in this configuration is not my own, fully, but it is the action I am responsible for. My being emerges in response to a call both from within and from outside, like sound, dissipating again in time. I exist, briefly, in a state of surrender, and this vulnerability demands care, the kind engendered in the state of listening, which actor training privileges. It's not an inherently "nice" or "good" state of being, but a turning toward the other that demands everything of the senses and throws time outside the capitalist system of use-value. We are interested in generating dialogue, not manufacturing skilled artists as products or generating theater works that act merely as expressions of institutional authority.

Alterity and Difference

The acting program at the Norwegian Theater Academy at Østfold University College teaches foundations of acting while actively questioning technique and experimenting with contemporary approaches to theater and performance. We teach actors who work in a variety of media, text being only one of many potential scenic materials in a process. Training at NTA feels at times like a crisis of self: the work is not constructed to simply validate or help solidify one's comfort with the known world. The skills one acquires through this education can be described as a highly tuned awareness of the possibilities of theater and its collaborative mechanisms, including awareness of the role of audiences. The education does not aim to elevate the cult of the individual performer, nor does it idealize utopian ensemble. Workshops in diverse performance practices confront students with challenges that expand the notion of the self while also teaching ensemble problem solving skills—yet simultaneously deconstruct ideals in both. Visuality, sound, and other scenographic expressions play a large role in the dramaturgical process and inform performers' approaches via sensory intertwining. The senses are activated in every practice to ally the performer with a space, continually, through workshops with dramaturgies formed by and experimenting with the interactive qualities of breath, sound, listening, rhythm, partnering, objects, texts, and other materials.

In addition to theater productions and workshops, students engage in daily or weekly skill-based activities that familiarize them with their breathing, their anatomy (both imagined and experienced), and their sonic potential by way of text work, singing, yoga, contact improvisation, and dancing. The overlap of different approaches and cultural views often challenge the foundations of the very skills they are learning, so the notion of one true path or "way" is exchanged for something more fluid. NTA values the wisdom of rhythm and breath, as both have the ability to communicate various archives movement, text, and song forms are crucial to experience, and arrive from a range of sources. If training actively upsets the familiar and introduces competing rhythms, or other "centers" of breathing or movement, we may be able to challenge the stability of the "self" and call the human being out of her home and into a broader relationship with space. Singing practice is yet another study area joining our expansive, sensory approach: students work with musicality and embodiment through a wide range of song and sound sources.[2]

---

2   Extended vocal technique is regularly taught in various settings and is one of the influential practices that inform the expressive landscape at NTA.

Responsive Listening

Challenging actors with the unfamiliar—through confrontations with various aesthetic environments, tasks, compositions, and games—consistently engages the actor's responsiveness. This is not an easy process. "Deep play"[3] is a crucial element in the devising process. High expenditures of energy and experimental risk often operate without immediate return; for this reason, we articulate that failure is a necessary step in the maturation process of any performing artist. Laboratories and projects draw from a wide-ranging network of international artists who work theatrically, for example, with texts, sound, media composition, ensemble-devising processes, and choreographic methods. The workshops are curated to confront students with various working methods and alternative ways of conceiving the role of artistic practice in life. They come face-to-face with processes that demand from them precisely what they do not know how to do, or who to be. Confirmation of results, critical support, and feedback therefore need to be given in context, as a response to specific spaces and aims, though never in generalized terms (e.g. *good* or *bad* acting, "believability"). Reflection on the results, then, is a responsibility shared by student and teacher; it's a critical means to carry forward knowledge, methodologies, and values discovered in the practical research on both sides. Acting students do however repeatedly meet an artist's process as a direct challenge to their own need to completely understand and "know" the

---

3   From Clifford Geertz's *Interpretation of Cultures*, in his "Notes on a Balinese Cockfight," where he applies Jeremy Bentham's concept of "deep play." By this he means play "in which the stakes are so high that it is, from his utilitarian standpoint, irrational for men to engage in it at all." From the perspective of artists who value play it is the intensity of this risk and its ability to heighten potentially transformative (or disappointing) experiences that confirms, somehow, the meaning and resonance of group action.

process. Knowledge is a critical and tenuous product: it is not always the goal of an experience. The pursuit or illusion of knowledge can in fact close down the possibility for communication. One could ask, rather, "What is otherwise than knowledge?"—especially considering an art form based on responsive relations to people in public space. Contemporary theater practices offer a space to also resist the "knowledge imperative" of institutions, offering instead what Katherin Busch refers to as a "poetics of knowledge,"[4] or perhaps what Bataille in his book *Inner Experience* refers to as "nonknowledge": something like the burst of experience in the present moment of encounter. In this burst, the material outcome is contextual, sensorial, and embodied, emerging in relation. Learning is a reflection on and communication of seemingly ineffable experience (rather than only the pursuit of knowledge or representation systems). Attention to "nonknowledge" reshapes how we approach cultural critique and evolving perceptions of how expenditures of time and space influence people.

Acting training can confront and destabilize the idea that there is an authentic self which can be trained to do theater a particular way; there is no single, correct, unified "I" the education is trying to serve or produce, but rather asks students to remain in question throughout a rigorous practice of tangible and practical *seeking*. Working without a single grand instructional method demands the acting

---

4   Busch articulates a shared critical stance towards knowledge production in academia, where the demand for systems and useable knowledge products reflects a problematic market economy influencing research-based creative fields. She writes: "[I]n view of a steadily growing knowledge imperative, it is necessary to recall the theoreticians who refuse to restrict themselves to functioning as suppliers of knowledge, who view knowledge itself with great skepticism, and who see even their own theories as an inherent practice of knowledge criticism." I similarly see those who teach acting practice to hold a critical relationship to technique.

student be a thinking, curious person, unsure about the outcome of their experimentation.

Questioning Technique

Coming out of a century of theater manifestos and conflicting directorial styles, acting technique as a product of education has gone through many circular developments, with multiple interpretations and cults, each with their own living or dead charismatic leaders. It should be said that what it means to "act" or "perform" well in the European or American context changes with economic and cultural shifts. International trends might be critically described as not so subtly borrowed (even pilfered) styles, stories, tools, and vocabularies from other cultures and heralded as "new," or imperial "discoveries." There is nothing innocent about the history of actor training or its role in institutions. The fetish of the "new" and "yet unseen genius" drives a certain kind of art practice within a capitalist model, which is problematic: in some cases, institutions are inviting students to submit themselves to a physical, social, and psychological process that analyzes their personal habits and emotional tendencies along critical lines better suited to trends in the art market. Acceptance into an acting school is viewed as a stamp of approval signifying "natural talent" and symbolizing readiness to be shaped into a useful, consumable commodity. This sentiment is something to resist. A reflective and conscious theater education cannot promise new and improved *selves* as the end result of contemporary actor training, nor can it succeed by focusing training on a fixed notion of what it means to "become an actor."

We must, rather, lead students in a collaborative discovery of creative tools, methods, and potentials for the theater—demonstrating a set of shared values based on communication through trial and error, repetition and research. This begins by being curious about the "bad habits" students typically bring to their education. Students can learn from their own postures as much as we can train them. Institutions are responsible for teaching historicized critical discourse around the art forms being taught so students can critique and collaborate on the shape and direction of training. It is our students who lead us into "new" territory, which is sometimes discovered to be "old," and this circuit of recycling, rediscovery, trade, and re-invention can be a conscious, critical relationship with history and productivity. The appearance of any actual "new" material is perhaps what we refer to as the "unknown": a core aspect of live art and presence. *We are here together now, something unpredictable and surprising can and will happen.* This is invited. Education might not teach people to know what is unpredictable in live encounter, but at NTA we aim to teach artists to provoke its appearance. We demand an ethics protecting the unscripted relational experiences at the center of theater. To preserve a space for the unknown is to resist inscribing upon the actor a certain finished, commodified, or systematized "self," one that is sculpted, constructed, or shaped as a mechanism of interpretation. Instead, our education seeks to strengthen and support the surprise, the yet-to-be resonance that activates the potential in the human being. By fortifying the student with material tools, critical questions, and space for developing responsive, sensory musicality, acting students acquire a wider mobility. They develop the ability to listen well enough to collaborate and respond—to co-creators, audiences, architectures, landscapes, literatures—without foreclosing further listening. This is not "a technique," but a process of acquiring and inventing context-specific skills that can also be dropped and re-engaged in time.

Liminality and Self

An alternative to the convention of character emerged in the postmodern performance context: "performance of self," as in everyday life. This also references a theoretical discourse arriving from Erving Goffman's text of the same name. The interest in performing the real, via playing oneself, has already informed several generations of actors. But what are we asking when we claim to simply perform the "self," when the self is not at all a singularity or even wholly available as a knowable object, out of relation with history, place, or alongside other people? Can we really work with such an idea in our training when it is clearly been destabilized by critical theory? How can I train to perform my "self"? How can I do anything else?

I raise this issue to articulate a way of thinking about the concept of "self" inside contemporary actor training (not to detail methods of self-scripting). One of the inspiring principles we might use to describe the training process at NTA is the theory of *liminality*, brought into performance studies by Victor Turner and his work with ritual studies. Liminal is a term taken from the root word *limen*, which Richard Schechner describes as "a threshold or sill, an architectural feature linking one space to another—a passageway between places rather than a place in itself. A *limen* is often framed by a *lintel*, which outlines the emptiness it reinforces. In performance theory, *liminal* refers to 'in-between' actions or behaviors…" (67).

Liminality is a well-known principle in performance

and theater studies and is used in a variety of fields.[5] The liminal as a concept is very useful when thinking not only about performance practice, but as a space for the idea of self in actor training. We do not view the actor as a concrete, known entity. (Just as the person in society experiences themselves as both strange and familiar.) Neither are we playing only with the notion of the fragmented subject, but rather something more like the transitional space well described in the definition of liminal. We can think of the actor's work as play within that space, for sure, but must also consider that the actor herself is such a space; she is full of potentials and unknowns, temporary transformations and full-on becomings. The actor is always wrestling with the space between "me/not me," or throwing out the dialectic altogether, even offstage. What remains concrete is the frame: the limen itself as described above, realized as the materiality of the body, the vibration of senses, an expressive vocal instrument. In an effort not to overly fetishize the actor's body, we also create work where the actor can be corporeally "absent" and yet remain an essential agent in a space. The materiality of experience and the sensory landscape of the actor is but a base tool for experimentation and partnering with other human beings. For this reason, the liminal space is a necessary ethos of our training, where the intensification of the senses meets the potential for encounter. In relation to a text, the actor performs a set of tasks, actions, gestures, sounds, and supporting dramaturgical perspectives without resolving who the "I" is, instead exploring a range of potential personhoods. The frame of this continuum could also be

---

5   See Susan Broadhurst's research in her book *Liminal Acts*, for example.

thought of as a slide or a range, from "acting" to "not acting," evoking Michael Kirby's influential research on matrixed and non-matrixed performances.[6] The range of potential Kirby articulates is explored without necessarily relying on knowledge of "who I am" or "why I am who I am"—rather, I interact with the precariousness of experience. What unfolds is a collaboration with time in relation to text, character, a partner, space. In the act of composition, I can critique and reshape my own behavior as action.

Relation and Meaning

Our education aims to generate a vocabulary of spatial orientation. We ask performers to listen, as a primary action. Performer approaches adjust and shift in the moment of collaboration; they do not ally themselves with a "proper technique," but develop in response to the situation at hand. Listening is not about privileging one form of aesthetic input/output over another, be it noise or poetry. Articulation of sensory experience means bringing awareness to the performing moment—the timbre of sounds, the taste of words, the color of light—and making something with them. We also play with synaesthetic tendencies by tasting color in words and describing the temperature of sounds. None of these sensations need to be translated to psychological scores to be effective.

Jean-Luc Nancy, in his text *Listening*, draws our attention to listening as a curiosity and a way into caring for the open materiality of experience. He calls for a space of relation that is not about trading in coded meaning or brilliant ideas, but in the already available resonance of

---

6   *On Acting and Not Acting*, Michael Kirby.

the senses and shared spatial experience. This resonance is of great importance to our practice as theater makers and precedes the demand to only construct easily translatable worlds. Listening demands a suspension in time and care for that which is unknown, but given as material, if only ephemerally. Listening is not just attending to the words of the other, but to the gift of sound itself.

One might think of intensification of the senses as learning dynamic, spatial improvisation. We play with the potential musicality in all expressions, without relying on meaning or interpretation, yet still investigating relation. Meaning makes itself evident locally in different ways, without our signature. It precedes us and disappears. We do not have to "create" it or represent it. One illustration from metaphysics on the way in which relation generates both tender and dangerous material can be drawn from philosopher Emmanuel Levinas, where the notion of sensory encounter is crystalized as an ethical relation: whenever the face speaks, "the first content of expression is the act of expression in itself" (51). The face of the other demands response, and this demand is at the root of drama. Attending the face of the other—i.e. *listening*—draws up a world of responsive sensory material and improvisational problems for the actor while generating interesting crises onstage. Actors must learn to play with the flexibility of text, voice, body, and the rhythm of interacting with the space or a partner as part of their research, even in more rigorous compositions. In the best examples, this produces a state of intense, live collaboration with all the elements of the stage.

Acting students at NTA are also trained to respond with sonorous improvisation in their actions. A text or performance score may be, for example, playfully perforated through subtle awareness of its potential musicality. This can take the form of rhythmic intervention, tonal shifts, or playing with breath, as Electa Behrens and Camilla Eeg-Tverbakk elaborate on in their essays in this book. The actor responds creatively to the moment with improvisation, at every level a kinetic response, not in a frozen format but as a flexible dialogue. This responsiveness is valued far beyond any notion of one's perfect execution of a task or clarity of so-called "meaning." That said, our improvisation is intense enough (and scoring, choreography, and repetition practiced enough) that we can expect our actors' compositional choices to be dramaturgically rooted and reflective of invested research.

Our Approach and Intentions

Training at NTA seeks to enable actors to be responsive to a space, to know what's going on in a room and relate to it, both in terms of technical data (light, sound, sensory material) but also in terms of its live potential. An actor in our education does not have to be interested in politics or political art, but must be conscious of the implications of his or her actions, both on the human and non-human scale. Acting education at NTA asserts no expectation that the actor become more or less believable, or selfless, or that he or she becomes "a better person" after having experienced the process of acting. These are but peripheral qualities we might experience. We are much more interested in how the repeated challenge of being confronted with "that which is other than you" makes for a more interesting, playful, and dangerous stage, one that can better deal with the future potentials of theater more concretely.

Yielding to the Unknown

Contemporary theory on performance articulates in a rich language ways of conceiving the actor inside a range of postmodern and post-dramatic theater processes so varied that each cannot be summarized here. The intention of this essay is not to situate or outline actor-training history, but to reflect on some principles informing our acting program at Norwegian Theater Academy/Østfold University College. This reflection is a perspective directly connected to this author's leadership period at NTA. It is worthwhile to note, however, the historical influences in our educational thinking over the long term, ranging from Bertolt Brecht and Antonin Artaud to Hans Thies-Lehmann, Michael Kirby, and Richard Schechner, who's canonical statuses demonstrate that a critical line of inquiry into acting methodologies is nothing new. Phillip Zarrilli's book *Acting (Re)Considered* is an excellent example of a resource that reflects on the discourses of the contemporary field and their historicization. (Zarrilli has been a guest teacher at the school.) Contemporary training that relies on the legacy of key figures like Jacques Lecoq, Jerzy Grotowski, Sanford Meisner, or Michael Chekhov, for example, has certainly impacted teachers working with our students, but we do not hew to nor endorse any of these traditions specifically. Many key figures in the fields of postmodern dance and music/sound art have taught at NTA; both fields are deeply connected to our work with actors, particularly in regards to text. The methodologies of influential artists and companies such as Robert Wilson, Kelly Copper and Pavol Liška of Nature Theater of Oklahoma, Sxip Shirey, Bianca Casady of CocoRosie, Heiner Goebbels, Romeo Castellucci, Herbert Fritsch, Tim Etchells and Forced Entertainment, Jay Scheib, Louise Höjer, Tino Sehgal, Joshua Sofaer, Ong Keng Sen,

Responsive Listening

Edit Kaldor, Hans van den Broek, Frank Vercruyssen and tg STAN, Goat Island, Wooster Group, Kirsten Dehlholm and Hotel Pro Forma, Baktruppen, Verdensteatret, Verk, Alan Lucien Øyen and Winter Guests, Xavier Le Roy, and Meg Stuart, for example, inform the artists and dramaturgies of many of our workshops and projects. Many of the above artists have also taught for us.

At NTA, we have built an education around the notion of an unknown "center." This moving, transformative space is generated through our deep relationship with theory and mixed practices. This, we feel, is a generous and exciting response to the long history of styles and critiques we have inherited. We have not chosen one master to follow, but allow for the polyphonic and polyvocal, including resonances of modern and contemporary critiques of the theater, music, and visual arts, where practices and methodologies move in and out of focus in varying durations and intensities. We also do not place the actor at the center, but challenge each student to preserve that space for the work itself, in what ways they see fit. This does not mean the actor is unimportant; on the contrary, we envision and work within the idea of actor-as-creator. What or who they are changes with the work they choose to create, and through the ensembles they create and disband. What happens after graduation can be witnessed by our students' many performances, installations, theater plays, and events appearing in Norway and on the international stage. In short, their work speaks for itself.

References

Arendt, Hannah. *The Human Condition*. Chicago and London: University of Chicago Press, 1958. Print.

Bannerman, Adelaide. "Shaivistic Reverberations; Exchanges between Adrian Piper and Adelaide Bannerman." *International Review of African American Art* 21.3 (2007): 27-33. Print.

Bataille, Georges. *Inner Experience*. Albany: State University of New York, 1988. Print.

Busch, Kathrin. "Artistic Research and the Poetics of Knowledge." *Art and Research* 2.2 (2009). Print.

Geertz, Clifford. *The Interpretation of Cultures: Selected Essays*. New York: Basic, 1973. Print.

Jaeger, Suzanne M. "Embodiment and Presence: Ontology of Presence Reconsidered." *Staging Philosophy: Intersections of Theater, Performance, and Philosophy*. Eds. David Krasner and David Z. Saltz. Ann Arbor: University of Michigan Press, 2006. 122-141. Print.

Kirby, Michael. "On Acting and Not-Acting," *The Drama Review* 16.1 (1972): 3-15. Print.

Levinas, Emmanuel. *Totality and Infinity: An Essay on Exteriority*. Trans. Alphonso Lingis. Pittsburgh: Duquesne University Press, 1969. Print.

Marion, Jean-Luc. *The Erotic Phenomenon*. Trans. Stephen E. Lewis. Chicago and London: University of Chicago Press, 2006. Print.

Schechner, Richard. *Performance Studies: An Introduction*. New York: Taylor & Francis, 2006. Print.

On Scenography

Serge von Arx

Scenography as such does not exist. It is agency, consisting of the invisible relationships between spatially and temporally active constituents. It is a catalyst, rendering the hidden visible, or obscuring what we believe to see and know. A space is only the starting point of an avalanche set to occur in the spectators' imaginations. What exists inside things, behind things, and in-between things is more relevant as the immediate appearance of a space beset with objects. Scenography is ephemeral, yet must always refer back to something, be it a text, a piece of music, a movement, an object, or a topic. There is no scenography without a linking anchor, and it is the anchor's position in relation to a referent notion that creates its inherent dialogue. The volume, color, and spirit of this dialogue are the scenographer's tools. Scenography's main concern, though, is potentiality; relationships are set as frames around an unknown, to be filled by the spectators' imaginations. This makes the scenographer an architect of the illusory, defining space by adding or removing components; in this, the scenographer takes charge of an emptiness, a void, but one so "loaded" that it is constantly on the brink of exploding or imploding. The scenographer does not create new worlds, but rather creates a vibration in space using critical thought, reflecting on the decomposition and recomposition of realities. The notion of the "new" becomes obsolete when one transcends time-based characteristics, moving from the diachronic to the synchronic. Everything is already available; existing relationships are merely reshaped, redefined.

Performance is inherently bound to our physical condition as human beings. While most human activity strives to change our environment even by artificially expanding, accelerating, and enhancing our bodies, we remain locked up in our unchangeable somatic condition. This is where performance comes in as a linking intermediary. We perceive performances with all senses; the articulate balance between the visual, the acoustic, the haptic, and even the olfactory represents the compositional aim of a performing artist. While in most other art fields there is a clear focus on one or the other sensorial aspect, in the performing arts the artist intrinsically operates with the coherence of those respective constituents. This holistic character makes performance not only more easily accessible for everyone but can also be of referential interest to a broad field of cultural industries. Performance takes its essence from our everyday reality; the present and past worlds constitute its vocabulary. The artistic agent insists on decomposing and de-contextualizing our environment and history, and subsequently recomposing and re-contextualizing it. The according levels of fragmentation and re-relation represent the creative act.

Architecture is, like theater and music, a *time-based* art form. But in contrast to music and theater, where the artwork consists of a clear definition of the evolvement in time, architecture merely *frames* the time. The architect, rather, creates the *potential* for a visitor to experience a work, unfolding upon his or her own *free will*. We have the freedom to determine how we move through a city: we can choose where to go, how fast to go, where to look, what to interact with—but only to some degree, as that freedom is restricted by more or less clearly defined frames. And it is those very frames of which an architect or scenographer's work consists. While architecture usually follows functional, practical, legal, or in general more rational criteria, it is theater that turns architecture into scenography. (I am using the often confusing and culturally varying term "scenography" in its essential meaning of "writing space or stage," expanding it beyond mere stage design and into the realms of exhibition design, art in the public environment, etc., which is how we understand and teach it at the Norwegian Theatre Academy.) Maybe one could say scenography is architecture that inheres a clear *dramaturgical* momentum, architecture as occasion, referring to the full complexity of what is meant by dramaturgy. In this simplified context we might use "dramaturgical" to refer to a story or dramatic composition following one or more distinct paths along a timeline of more or less defined structures and properties. In most works of the performing arts these stories are linear and realistic, but they can be surrealistic, concrete, or even abstract. In whatever way one reads dramaturgy, it is an open practice, and allows for different interpretations by the performers, even if the timely development of the performance itself, as witnessed by the audience, evolves in a linear setting.

Scenography inherently concerns itself with nonlinear, spatial storytelling, not as an option but fundamentally, according to its inner structure. Architecture is experienced as it unfolds in space, according to the moving body and changing light. An architect or a scenographer's main tool is *materialization*—building spatial limits, fixed or movable ones, transparent, translucent, or opaque ones, using colors and surfaces, each constituent reacting differently to light, sound, touch. It is on purpose that I am blurring a differentiated approach to both fields, as in their essence architecture and scenography are one in the same. However, architecture can be non-materialized as well. Architecture can be created through music, through scent, or even through a change of temperature. Scenography, then, is sensory storytelling expressed through architecture, storytelling one experiences with one's whole body in space. It merges the inherent realness of architecture and the inescapable artificiality of theater, and it is this intrinsic collision that nurtures scenography as an intriguing chimera.

In my eyes there is a big lack within contemporary architecture: that of the scenographical as described above, the lack of theater, of theatricality, of nonlinear storytelling that respects the potential for new stories to take place. We have to find our way back to utilizing the city as our main stage of everyday life. The city must allow for scenographical events to take place, rather than attempt to create events with architecture.

To observe and listen—and perhaps this is the most important point for us to teach art students—if you carefully listen to and observe what is happening around you, you realize everything you need is already available. Instead of constantly trying to create the new, as we have created so much already, which we are about to succumb to, I think our focus should foremost be on what we have already created, while identifying ways to deal with those elements—not to conserve what is there, but to progressively dismantle it. This doesn't mean taking a *phase admirative* approach, a gaze in admiration of what we have accomplished, but observing the resulting outcomes, the consequences of what we have created. If the reason we create art is to "ask questions," then the essence of the work lies in what we receive back, in terms of dialogue. And theater is always a dialogue; it does not exist without an audience. When constantly creating, we risk not perceiving what has already been done; this is the point when the artist's responsibility, as Arthur Miller suggests, lies in reminding society "what it has chosen to forget."

Art for me is about framing the unknown, finding the perfect balance between establishing a frame while keeping the limits as open as possible. Be it a theater piece, a sculpture, a poem, or a film, it is the unknown which is filled by our imagination, and hence what makes the reading of any art work personal, allowing us to relate it. If I cannot relate to it, it is irrelevant to me. It is essential that the artist insinuate a bridge between the work and the spectator. I believe this is true for all the arts, but especially for architecture. Where a spatial definition allows for only one way to go and look, it is the architect's hegemonic obtrusion. The architect, rather, should contribute to the fields of gravity of public space. The theater director, on the other hand, juggles the constituents of theatrical work—the space, the text, the music, and other elements of a performance. If he or she begins to fill that fragile unknown area between—the "public space" within a performance—while defining how things are lined up on a timeline, the potential for our imagination begins to decrease. The theater director should weave the components into each other while still maintaining a space for the unknown, just as the architect should do in the city. I've often thought stage directors should spend some time working in urban development, while architects experience work in the theater—if this happened, perhaps the divisions between them might begin to overlap more; the beneficiaries of this experience would be the audience.

On *Playing* a Text

Camilla Eeg-Tverbakk

"Sound is acting."
John Cage

The French sociologist and philosopher Henri Lefebvre has written a short book about rhythm analysis appropriately called, *Rhythmanalysis*. In the book he presents a rhythmic approach to life; everything has a rhythm because everything is a composition consisting of words, movement, intensity, sound, form, images, etc. All subjects, all characters, all bodies are therefore one of many rhythms accumulating into the bigger picture. Seeing the world as rhythm also emphasizes the connection between all things, sentient beings and materials. Polyphony is perhaps the most realistic way of portraying reality, if that is a goal, and it all starts in our own bodies. The body is like a metronome, and all other rhythms are measured in relation to it.

The quote above from John Cage is as relevant when inverted. In this essay I will argue for the fact that as much as sound is an action or that sound creates action, acting is also sound! Traditionally in theater and acting there is a tendency to focus on the meaning of sound. When text and words are uttered on stage, we are less interested in the musicality of language and more interested in the mental interpretations we make personally and culturally of those sounds. In my work at the Norwegian Theatre Academy, teaching acting students the many ways of treating and relating to a text in front of an audience, the focus lies more on the act of relation/relating than the act of interpreting what the various relations at play mean. Interpretation is almost impossible to avoid, which is why it is important to draw attention away from development and analysis of specific interpretations of a text. For a multiple and complex space of interpretation to exist, opening spaces of relation in a performing situation becomes an ethical issue, not only between artist/performer and audience, but between performer, *text*, and audience. The ethical aspect comes into play upon examining what can be understood as a colonization of a text, which the artist/performer acts out after taking ownership of a specific interpretation of a chosen material. What is at stake here is the power relations between the artist—performers, dramaturge, director—the material, and the audience. How do we relate to the chosen material we work with, be it text, movement material, scores, objects, or scenographic materials?

Humans attempt to capture things by defining them, culturally and through language. Object-Oriented Philosophy and New Materialism offer discourses on the ways in which we, as humans, relate to things—each with their own critique of anthropomorphism. The idea is to look at, listen to, and relate to things understood as material with a life of their own—or rather to see and listen to the vibrations generating a certain kind of life and meaning without our interference. Archaeologist Ian Hodder writes in his book *Entangled: An Archaeology of the Relationships between Humans and Things* of the ways in which humans and things create each other's worlds through a reciprocal dependency, thus human existence is "thingly." He continues, "Things do have a primary agency, not because they have intentionality but because they are vibrant and have lives and interactions of their own" (68). My approach with performers is to regard text as a "thing" that materializes and creates reality through its mere uttering, in a space where someone receives and listens to the sounds. This obviously draws on J.L. Austin's understanding of performativity in his famous lectures "How to Do Things with Words," delivered at Harvard University in 1955. Austin points to the power of language to make things happen, creating reality through the iteration of specific words in specific contexts of power. This builds on Cage's quote that sound is acting. Within the context of teaching acting students, though, my concern is with treating texts as materials that carry their own meaning, partly hidden from the person speaking it, with the idea that performer and audience explore and move into active relation with a text in the moment of performance, without prior fixed modes of interpretation.

Text-thing

To see text as "thing" is to explore what text does. What is it, in each particular text, that makes it come into being as a thing, and how does a performer's encounter with a text influence her or his presence in relation to an audience? When the "thinging of the thing" takes place through presencing, nearness is at work, says Martin Heidegger in his famous essay "The Thing." To explore a text and how it becomes a thing means to see the text as a relational tool through which proximity, intimacy, trust, power, violence, distrust, and distance is played out. Silvia Benso, who draws on the work of Heidegger and Emmanuel Levinas, explores our relationship with things as an ethical encounter with alterity in her book *The Face of Things: A Different Side of Ethics*. To relate to things as alterity, Benso argues, is to question the position of the 'I' as an absolute beginning taking space in the encounter with the Other. She speaks of things as having many faces, what she calls "facialities," of which some are hidden to us. What we need to do, she argues, is enter into relation with things through tenderness. Tenderness with a text implies touch, attention, and patience. But how can a text-thing be explored and touched? Through listening, through being conscious of how words are formed and shaped via breath, touching and vibrating through our vocal cords sounds touch the tongue and lips as words are constructed. The point is to relate to the text-thing in a way where you cannot fix it in a specific position to a self. Each time one performs it one has to be sensitive to one's position towards it. Where am I today in relation to the thing? Am I far away, am I close, am I under it or above it; is it fluctuating; can I reach it at all, am I able to touch it today; and if so, how does it feel at the moment of performing it? It is a spatial relationship, where the performer discovers the text together with an audience in the moment.

Rhythm and Body

Rhythms and body are the basis for acting. For an actor it means to find play in/with movement, pulse, and breath. It is with these instruments that an actor can choose to *play* the text, by letting the text resonate with, and be in step with the body's own rhythms, which always relate to and engage with other rhythms outside the actor's own body. This is the core understanding of rhythmic perspective.

Actors and theater directors know what it means to play a text. Traditionally, it means interpreting the text, then, based on that interpretation, creating a character whose situation and psychology the actor can empathize with: relating the lines to one's own experience and drawing on that sense experience to trigger a full range of the actor's emotions. It entails a meeting between the actor's mental life and the imaginary psychological life of the character. We know this understanding of what it means to play a text from the classical text-based theater of the late nineteenth century, mostly advocated by the writings of Konstantin Stanislavski, and what has developed into the "Stanislavski method," better known as "method acting." This is a way of "playing" where the word 'play' is used in the sense of pretending. It is a method that reflects that era's prevailing understanding of the subject as Sigmund Freud, in particular, wrote about it, claiming that there is a hidden subtext that expresses the real 'I' in all communication. This 'I' is more or less hidden, and what is being said represents different reflections of this cloaked subject. Here text is a kind of *surface* to be analysed and interpreted in order for one to access a subject's underlying *core* and *truth*—the unearthing defines and shapes the hidden landscapes of the text. This approach presupposes a meeting between two clearly defined subjects: the actor and the character in the text. But if an actor does not want to take a psychological approach to a text, what tools are available?

Unlike the above approach, a contemporary understanding of subject and character is less well defined and final. It is more fluid, more shifting, and in a constant process of change; something that feels true one moment may not the next. Contemporary notions of subjectivity allow for a different kind of encounter with a text. Words no longer reflect a unique, clearly defined subject, but become utterances that give voice (sound) to social, political, and economic positions. The text becomes then a material that the actor explores together with the audience, a medium enabling dialogue. Within this interpretative framework, one way of approaching text is to listen to what takes place in the encounter—between one's own body, the words, the other bodies listening in the room, as well as the room itself. This process of listening to rhythms makes it possible to share texts and have them understood separately within the framework of sound and musicality.

Words as Actions

Spoken text has become an intrinsic part of contemporary dance performances. Dancers work with text on stage in a way similar to how they work with movement. It is less about interpretation and more about performing action. Actors can learn from this focus by pointing beyond the performing subject, where it is the performer's task to portray or present other voices, rather than specific characters. In my experience dancers are good at communicating text within this paradigm because they are used to working with rhythms, tempo, intensity, atmospheres, timbre, etc., which they naturally anchor in their own bodies. Movement helps them not only to remember the text but also to place it, so to speak, on the boundary between the inside and the outside, i.e. on the skin. Thus the task does not constitute a meeting between text and a specific subject. Instead, the text is liberated, and can flow out into the room, allowing the audience access to a larger space for interpretation without having to relate to the actual subject on the stage or to the performer's or director's fixed interpretations. This requires an open, unprejudiced, and trustful attitude on the actor's part, where his or her presence within the play of and in conjunction with the text becomes the continuous practice of exploring the text in the moment, here and now. It is not about deciding on an interpretation to be communicated, but rather exploring how text works through one's self today, how it vibrates in a person. Instead of having the audience spend time looking for interpretations and meanings worked out in advance, a dialogue is created. A rhythmic or musical approach provides one the opportunity to hear a text in the broadest sense: the concrete meaning of the words, the physical expression, the vibration or movement that is triggered by the relationship between text, body, and voice. These different layers relate to each other in a polyphonic structure, which extends the possibility for a polyphonic formation of meaning.

A polyphonic structure consisting of different sign systems can be, it should be said, a confusing experience. But it is precisely this confusion that creates the democratic space within which audience members, in fellowship, can arrive at their own interpretation. It is a space that gives room to limitless readings of a material with the potential to influence ways in which we think, feel, and behave. It is a space that accommodates difference. In *Performance Research* Kai van Eikels calls it *synchronisation*, which he believes can replace the idea that fellowship means being together in one uniform space. Instead, he points to a process where we attune individual rhythms to each other, the rhythms flowing back and forth between us. But this requires a medium that can communicate information in all directions between everyone involved. A dramatic text can be this medium. This form of synchronisation is temporary and allows for differences, so we do not end up with one common rhythm, which would represent dictatorship of a single idea being forced upon the listeners instead of the democratic space of the polyphonic structure.

Listening

Listening is necessary in order for both performer and audience to achieve a musical approach to the scenic experience. Listening, not just with the ears, but with all the senses. In his book *Listening*, the French philosopher Jean-Luc Nancy asks:

> What does it mean for a being to be immersed entirely in listening, formed by listening or in listening, listening with all his being? [...] What secret is at stake when one truly *listens*, that is, when one tries to capture or surprise the sonority rather than the message? (4-5)

The answer to this lies, among other things, in the bodily experience of rhythms, which are perceived not only by the ear, but also by the eye, muscles, skin, nervous system. Nancy speaks about the concept of listening in which the subject is understood to be in a process of constant dissolution and reformation or deterritorializing and reterritorializing, as Deleuze and Guattari would have put it. Listening, for Nancy, is to be penetrated by spatiality and all that it contains. He also speaks of sonority, what he calls timbre and sense, when describing a certain kind of listening that searches for what precedes meaning. This sonority, which always surrounds us, is not yet given form or captured by meaning; it escapes language. This kind of listening is part of daily conversation: when we talk to each other the speaking travels so fast that we are often unable to immediately catch the meaning of all the words or understand their content. Attempting to hear what is spoken, we also listen for sonority, helped in its deciphering by what the other person transmits through his or her physical presence. We are listening on many levels simultaneously, noticing formations that have not yet appeared, but which are present as potentials, perhaps even sensing things none of us know are there.

Nancy calls this kind of listening "stretching the ear." The process involves striving for an interpretation that is not directly accessible, and requires care, inquisitiveness, a desire for intensification, and agitation. This is not a psychological approach to what is understood as "subtext" in classical theater, involving instead a completely different understanding of subject and character. It is a form of listening that is about relating to a "self" (one's own self and others') while recognizing a relationship that exists between all listeners. A "self" is something different from both character and "I"—it is less defined, more fluid. Listening to rhythm, music, or sound in the broadest sense means allowing oneself to be penetrated, and to a certain extent dissolved, into a broader state of becoming. Nancy describes this as follows:

> To listen is to enter that spatiality by which, at the same time, I am penetrated, for it opens up in me as well as around me, and from me as well as toward me: it opens me inside me as well as outside, and it is through such a double, quadruple, or sextuple opening that a "self" can take place. To be listening is to be at the same time inside and outside, to be open from without and from within, hence from one to the other and from one in the other. (14)

Responsive Listening

To practice the kind of listening Nancy describes above is not easy. It demands a paradigmatic shift in how we seek to understand ourselves and our connections in the world. It demands we pay our senses greater attention, and further consider movements that oscillate, like breath, between our body and the outside world. One artist who has been partially exploring this form of listening in her creative work is the American actress and playwright Anna Deavere Smith. She has worked for many years on a very specific form of documentary theater. She often addresses topical controversies, usually relating to racial conflicts in the US, such as the Rodney King case in Los Angeles in 1992, or the incident in Crown Heights, Brooklyn in 1991, when a black boy was killed by a car driven by a Hassidic Jew—as addressed by Deavere Smith's famous performance *Fires in the Mirror*. She endeavoured to illuminate this particular conflict by interviewing involved parties from contending sides with various points of view and using some of their stories for a series of staged monologues. What separates Deavere Smith from other playwrights is that her goal is not entirely to create empathy using the individual testimonies, addressing the purely emotional or psychological issues, but to shed light on the different social, political, and economic conditions surrounding their conflicts by partially focusing on the musicality of the language of her interviewees and capturing their rhythms, both in their speech and actions/gestures. She may start by concentrating on how a person breathes, and through this identify the rhythm of their speech. When this is combined with the rhythm of body movement and gesture, a picture of that person begins to emerge, reflecting aspects of their personal complexities and emotional lives without these aspects being explicitly analysed by the actor.

By focusing on the polyphonic rhythms—the rhythms of the body and speech vary and are not necessarily the same—the audience can see, or listen, in Nancy's sense of the word, in a more all-embracing way, without looking for a psychological reason behind the utterances. This approach allows greater room for interpretation. Deavere Smith does not seek to emphasize or problematize private motives. Instead, she wants to show the audience how power in the public domain is represented through language and body. Thus Smith sheds light on the myriad conditions that lead to conflict and influences how we deal with such conflicts. It is not the subjects' personalities and psyches that are interesting, but what they represent by dint of their role in society.

From an ethical perspective, it is very important to Deavere Smith's project to maintain a certain distance from her subjects. The goal is not to help viewers recognize similarities or likenesses between themselves and the characters, for purposes of recognition or identification, but rather to create a distance in which the actor becomes the medium, a body and a voice conveying the position and opinions of the person in question. Deavere Smith is not trying to understand, or claim that she can represent, someone's psyche—that would be a violation of, or, at best, an encroachment on, their integrity. By adopting a listening approach in the interview situation, and reproducing the interviewee's musicality, she endeavours to understand the interplay that takes place in the social fabric, the specific musicality and rhythm of conveyance. A character's rhythm is never constant, and depends upon the situation and topic of conversation. When Deavere Smith "plays" her interviewee in a performance, it is with a distance that also includes Deavere Smith as a listening journalist. When this text is "played," it allows room for the subject's articulated opinion, but also for Deavere Smith's individual, social, and political position as an African-American woman, as well as the positions and opinions of the entire audience. In allowing this, the portrayal opens a space for dialogue and discussion about race, gender, and power at many different levels.

Sharing Breath

When I work with acting students on a text and ask them to breathe deeply, they often find the challenge difficult, even confrontational. They feel vulnerable breathing deeply on stage. This is probably a matter of habit, but it tells us something about how, when people are asked to work consciously on their breathing, they are brought in contact with their feelings and also with a human vulnerability linked to the body's internal organs—the rhythms that keep us alive. It is these rhythms that make us alike, that put us in contact with a character and with the audience. I am not speaking of Deavere Smith's mimetic breathing, but of the performing subject's own breath—the one that reveals the actor, the one that sets physical and emotional energies in motion, causing the performer to lose control and expose that vulnerability. Working on breathing when working on a text means absorbing the words you have said, and letting the text vibrate or resonate in your body. Breathing increases circulation, which, in turn, moves us—physically, emotionally, and mentally. By breathing, we help give our feelings freer rein. The result will be something that takes place in the here and now, something that can surprise both the actors and the audience.

To play the text is to listen to it, to listen to my own speech, to explore it together with an audience: Integrating the words with my own and others' rhythms, and letting the text itself resonate, this creates meaning. To speak is already to listen, says Jean-Luc Nancy. Speaking is the text's echo, an echo of how the text has been created and written, and an echo that opens up the diversity of its possible meanings. Nancy says that this is not about the text's musicality, but about the music in the text. He emphasises how sound communicates what it is not possible to communicate: communication itself. Meaning a subject that communicates creates an echo of both its own self and the other. Communication, Nancy says, is not dissemination, but a form of participation or sharing that shapes subjectivity.

Playing – An Ongoing Practice

There is no difference between rehearsals and performing for an audience. Performing is the same practice as rehearsing. It is a continuous process. As this exercise of repeating words and actions evolves, a relationship grows between the text as thing-becoming-subject, and the performer as subject-becoming-thing. This practice opens up an ethical space of transformations, ambivalence, and difference. It is a love relationship and a practice. This relationship between performer and thing extends to affect the relationship between performer and audience. The invitation given by things through their silent presence and as witness of all human activity resists the I's voracity, autonomy, unlimited power, and mastery. The ethics of things, which Silvia Benso argues for, is a means to transcend ego and give up the authority of the normative position to its fullest extent. This process creates a dynamic, unfixed relationship always in motion. It is an attempt to relate ethically to the text as a living material, which is owned neither by performer, audience, nor author. Jean-Luc Nancy is concerned with "being-with-one-another" as that which gives meaning in itself. In our society, the production of meaning is a hot topic. Here, the proposal is to focus less on the topical, perhaps even to stop looking for meaning, because "being-*with*"—that is, being in circulation with everything—*is* meaning. To relate is meaning. We don't *have* meaning, says Nancy, we *are* meaning. To look for meaning is meaningless. Speaking, then, is an act of staying with and remaining in relation to, in order to maintain something that consists of sharing. Words open up spaces for audiences and performers to fill anew each time they are uttered. For the performers, the repetition is a new possibility to search further, to try each time to stay in vibrant relation with those hidden faces, the faciality of the thing, which is unspeakable and unrepresentable. Conversation or discourse is a way to sustain the "being-*with*," to make it (re)appear again and again, to make a world (re)appear and come into Being. It is like playing, as in children's play, a way to be with, hang out, and create and recreate the world anew in every moment, with friends and strangers, in order to bring the ever-changing subject into being.

References

Austin, JL, *How to Do Things with Words*. Cambridge: Harvard University Press, 1975. Print.

Benso, Silvia. *The Face of Things: A Different Side of Ethics*. Albany: State University of New York Press, 2000. Print.

Heidegger, Martin. *Poetry, Language, Thought*. New York: Harper Perennial Modern Classics, 2001 (1971). Print.

Hodder, Ian. Entangled: *An Archaeology of the Relationships between Humans and Things*. West Sussex: John Wiley & Sons, 2012. Print.

Nancy, Jean-Luc. *Listening*. New York: Fordham University Press, 2007. Print.

Van Eikels, Kai. "What Parts of Us Can Do with Parts of Each Other (and When): Some Parts of this Text." *Performance Research* 16.3 (2011): 2-11. Print.

Manifesto In Praxis:
Calling for a (Re)considered
Approach to Training
the Performer's Voice[1]

Electa Behrens

Voice training does not exist in a vacuum. It is created and develops in relation to changes in performance; as what needs to be trained changes, so does the training. The question is how fast and/or adequately do trainings adapt? Jacqueline Martin, in her 1991 comprehensive historical study, came to this conclusion:

> Although actor training has endeavoured to keep abreast of these changing attitudes to vocal delivery [...] it has been shown that the problems [...] seem to be of a much more complex nature [...] very few opportunities seem to have existed for experimentation of the nature which could encompass the kind of training necessary for contributing to the demands of the postmodern theatre. (192)

---

1   I use "(re)" in the sense that Phillip Zarrilli introduced in *Acting (Re)considered*: "For the actor, moments of (re)consideration are times when practice and thought crystallize in an insight which clarifies his or her (embodied) performance practice and technique" (2).

Manifesto in Praxis

At the Norwegian Theatre Academy, we have three voice pedagogues, each with their own area of expertise. We work alongside a curated program of workshops and original performances led by world-renowned artists. With a student body consisting of fewer than twenty students, we've created an intimate, dynamic, and flexible environment with an active feedback exchange between students and staff in regards to the interactions between "skill" trainings and the development of aesthetics occurring within a workshop context. The NTA has a unique ability to actively engage with the gaps that appear between "tried and true" voice methods and the boundary-pushing requirements of new performance work.

Before introducing some core ideas of the (re) considered direction I propose, I will first briefly catalogue some of these "gaps."[2] Trainings can be divided into three main models: the Traditional, the Universal and the Devised. Each has their strengths and weaknesses. The Traditional model, which is most common in drama schools, and is connected to text-based theater and naturalistic ideas of "acting," prioritizes the voice, but is limited in that it develops only a narrow range of the performers' expressive spectrum and does not help the performer shift between aesthetics, as it is based in very aesthetic-specific core ideas.

Most actors today are trained according to the one method favored by their particular teacher or school. Most often the specific approach is not taught in a conscious or critical process, but

---

2   This is a summary of a more detailed discussion which can be found in my PhD thesis: *VOCAL ACTION: From Training Towards Performance*, available from http://ethos.bl.uk.

is absorbed *experientially* by the student as a unique set of practices [...] Problems occur when [...] actors are asked to create performances utilizing techniques and stage conventions other than the ones in which they were schooled. These problems arise not merely because actors are unfamiliar with the alien conventions and techniques, but also because their performing identity has already been formed by the aesthetic they have unself-consciously absorbed in training. (Gordon 2)

The Universal model was introduced by practitioners such as Jerzy Grotowski and Eugenio Barba in the 1970s, and is based on the idea that there are certain "universal principles" at work beneath all aesthetics and cultures of performance (Barba 8). Utilizing this model can certainly train a vocally expressive performer, yet despite its claim of universality, it often locks performers within a narrow range of aesthetic expressivity, in much the same way the Traditional method does. Here the range of expression is derived not from "realistic acting" but is rather often characterized by an intensive physicality associated with "physical theater." While useful in developing certain skills and abilities, highly immersive, deep-level training of this sort can actually block the performer, as one's body literally becomes shaped by the training on a muscular level. As ballet dancers (due to the focus of their training on lightness, lines, and extension) often struggle to find the softness and grounding needed for African dance, Grotowski diaspora performers sometimes appear, for example, overly energetic in British-devised theater (as they are unable to modulate their learned, extended expressivity to the suit the down-played simplicity of the new form). More subtlety and specifically, in relation to vocal training, ideas of universality are often highly culturally coded, thus making them unhelpful within a multicultural working context. Voice pedagogue Tara McAllister-Viel, who works in Korea and the UK, writes:

> Concepts are dependent on cultural and discipline-specific concepts of the body. *Breath is not a universally understood physiological process* able to be reduced to lung function (object-body). Also, breath understood subjectively (subject-body) is equally problematic, in part because the "lived body" is heavily influenced by the sociocultural understandings of self and the place of body as self within praxis. [emphasis added] (McAllister-Viel, "(Re)considering" 173)

Neither the Traditional nor the Universal models include a well-reflected compositional training, which the Devised model offers, though often greatly ignores work on the physical voice. For example, in Oddey's *Devising Theatre: A Practical and Theoretical Handbook*, the voice is mentioned only fourteen times in 272 pages. In *Making a Performance: Devising Histories and Contemporary Practices* (Govan, Nicholson, Normington), it is mentioned only nine times in 215 pages. In most of these instances, the writer references the idea of the performer's creative rather than physical voice. This marginalization of vocal skills training is often due to limited rehearsal time, which leads to the prioritization of the creation of material over voice training, as well as a residual distrust of the voice as a function of text-based performance, a form from which the Devised model actively looks to separate itself.

Today there is a need for an approach embodied and compositional that addresses the multiplicity of existing approaches without becoming fragmentary. Building the structure of such a work is as much about the attitude towards work as the content of the training itself. It requires a new relationship between pedagogue and student and a new set of skills to be taught, including strategies of how to approach a training, how to *see* it for its functional aspects, how to negotiate ones own truth within a training model based on another idea of "truth," and how to take elements from one training method into another method. It is a proactive approach, as much about learning how to learn as the learning itself. Practically, it requires that the pedagogue take the training out of the well-used model of "a single student and teacher in the vacuum of a small room," so that voice teachers consistently engage students in working with different spaces, and to a greater extent include multiple notions of self within narratives of a "true voice." We must give students a vocabulary for working with the voice as a compositional element (i.e. learning to see their voice from the outside) and challenge them from the first day not to look to the teacher for the "right" answer, but rather cultivate and learn to articulate their own relationship to "vocal truth."

This is the training culture I promote in my work. In Table 1, I outline the criteria upon which I've founded my teaching and training. Table 2 catalogues some commonly held assumptions that underlie many voice practices today, and looks to uncover why they may no longer be helpful for the contemporary performer.

THE CONTEMPORARY PERFORMER MAY...	A PERFORMER'S TRAINING NEEDS TO...	
be both creator and performer of a work.	**01**	-teach vocal presence and the ability to work with vocal composition.
often work without a director.	**02**	-be collaborative, rather than have a hierarchical work ethic. -create a common vocabulary to be used for physical or vocal work, and allow for discussion of sound as a structural component versus a psychological one.
work within many different forms of performance.	**03**	-be based not in a single aesthetic, but rather work across forms. -be non-hierarchical; all vocal forms should be valued equally as potential performance material. (Work with text is not prioritized over work with pure sound, for example.)
arrive from any cultural or aesthetic background.	**04**	-not promote the idea of a "free" or "natural" voice as a starting point, but rather focus on the necessary voice, the one that responds adequately to the moment.
work in a variety of collaborative constellations with a variety of different economic limitations.	**05**	-be flexible, and can be adapted for solo, pair, or group work, all skill levels, and various rehearsal/training periods.

Table 1

"VOICE TRAINING SHOULD..."	WHY SHOULD THIS ASSUMPTION BE AVOIDED?
teach vocal skills such as range, resonators, articulation, pitch, blending, etc. as the *only* set of vocal values	-Concepts of skills are culturally bound. -"I saw some highly educated King's College choirboys demonstrate their aural acuity by repeating with their voice complex chromatic phrases played once at the piano. The same talented group was then presented with some "simple" tunes learned by novices in Java […] The choirboys were confounded by a division of the scale that evaded the concept of both tones and semitones, although found simple by Javanese children of half their age […] what may seem apt vocally in Cambridge may seem inept in Java." (Barker 3-4)
"warm-up" the voice	This idea artificially isolates one part of the work from the rest and places it in the fictional space of "not being the real thing"; an idea which has limited validity in many performance forms today. Secondly, it often results in performers not committing fully to the warm-ups and doing them automatically.
train one to "breathe correctly"	In most Western voice trainings, the breath is conceptualized and trained as a biological process. Breathing is thus seen as a skill which you can get good at. As McAllister-Viel made clear, this approach is culturally limited.
work to "free" or "open" the voice and promote the concept of a "good" voice	"Free," "open," and "good" are culturally bound concepts. An extreme example is *The Diagnosis and Correction of Vocal Faults*, where McKinney defines "good" and "bad" voices into very narrow technical boxes. This search for *openness/goodness*, which guides many of the leading vocal techniques in a Western context, leads to a great amount of stress put on realigning actors, fixing postural habits, and correcting breathing. This is, however, based on a Western concept of body-mind duality and the metaphor of the voice as machine (McAllister-Viel, "Voicing Culture" 427). Both of these images constrict the creation of voice exercises as well as the range of expressive choices the practitioner perceives as available to them.

Table 2

In Praxis

In the previous section, as a theoretician, I looked to briefly identify and outline the gaps in current voice trainings. In this following section, as a voice teacher, I will offer some (by no means exhaustive) practical examples of ways to move forward. It is crucial that this manifesto does not stand alone, a provocation without a proposal. It is always easier to critique than to suggest a solution, so I offer of my own strategies here in order to begin a concrete dialogue between pedagogues. At heart I am a teacher interested in people; I believe theory must support practice not simply dissect it. Let it be clear that this is a call for the (re)consideration of voice training, not a call to revolution. I have the greatest respect for the years and years of work that has gone into creating the voice methods that are available to today's performer. Yet I believe we must actively relate to the past, and I draw on what I have learned from my teachers every day. My proposal is not that the "vocal skills" championed in the West over the past fifty years be thrown out, but simply re-contextualized.

I will begin by signposting some organizing principles of my teaching, which may be relevant to other practitioners, starting with contextual structures that frame our work at NTA and then moving on to specific examples of exercises I use in training. Regardless of what trainings are employed, it is important to first create the conditions around the training, which acknowledge and embrace the reality of cultural multiplicity we live in today. It is only in this repeated, head-on convergence of methods that the real challenges of cross-discipline work appear.

At NTA, each of the three voice pedagogues comes from a different vocal tradition. For both students and pedagogues, the challenge of negotiating these different methods, which on the surface may in some moments appear contradictory, is not theoretical, but a lived experience—we teach the same students, often on the same day. In our attempts to understand the traditions relationally, we must shift the discourse from simplistic questions of "right" or "wrong" ways of using the voice to more challenging questions like "for what is this technique appropriate?" Teaching happens not only within each pedagogue's studio, but in the resonant space between. In this process, we deepen an awareness of our own individual praxis. It is often in the slippage between forms that new approaches and expressions are born.

Each method, or inclusionary technique, brings with it a language, one might even say a poetics, with which the pedagogue (with the best intentions) uses to help inspire the student. However, it is often within such evocative teaching language that ideological beliefs appear as singular truths (suggesting that there is only "one right way" to work). It is in these moments that one method can falsely appear to negate the realities of other methods and potentially confuse students. For example, in certain trainings it may seem inappropriate to ask for a mechanical explanation of what is going on in the body, whereas with other trainings the focus lies in explicitly replicating physiological movements with the voice. These two approaches are not necessarily contradictory; they are simply two ways to approach a task. In order to avoid the value judgments that are hidden in some training languages, I assert that the pedagogue should find a language for describing exercises that is performer-specific. Each exercise I present can be explained by four different general categories of description: there are those based on a psychological image/intention (e.g. you want to push him away with your voice); an abstract image/element (e.g. feel the fire growing in your tummy); a physical/kinaesthetic explanation (which describes the performers' embodied experience—though it is important to note that sometimes what is experienced is not always what *actually* happens in the body—e.g. draw the sound up from your feet); and the intellectual/technical (which describes what *actually* happens in the body—e.g. allow your ribs to open to the side and your diaphragm to release). The challenge of seeing each exercise from these different angles helps me eradicate any parasitic value judgements or assumptions that cloud the clarity of an exercise. As different students respond best to different forms of explanation and stimulation, having this rubric of categories in my head allows me to quickly assess a situation and respond appropriately to the performer in front of me. Using this approach, I train proactive performers to recognize the kind of language that stimulates them, so that they might hone their own training to their specific needs and personality, as well learn new ways to articulate to future collaborators what processes might help unlock their creative flow.

While the context of NTA provokes the negotiation between forms on a macro scale, my classes explore this process on the level of the exercise, which is a related but more exacting procedure. In practical sessions, I combine Traditional methods, such as support and articulation exercises devised by Kristin Linklater, with Universal techniques, such as structured sound improvisations. This approach of "mixing" techniques allows for embodied comparative research to take place within the performer.

Principles and practices inside of my body/voice can be understood in reference to each other; each tradition becomes an embodied context for learning the praxis of another tradition. Through trial and error as well as strategically designed interactions, the different trainings inside of me can interface. These combinations create different body knowledges from which I am able to develop alternative methods and models for training my voice. (McAllister-Viel, "(Re)considering" 174)

In this way the performer learns how to uncover the functionality of a method, its structuring principles, rather than pursue its forms only superficially, listening for "how it sounds." All work with sound (for the one who sounds) functions *as* some form of communication; it is a series of actions and reactions spurred by impulse.[3] The main difference between how communication is utilized in different aesthetics relates to time: the length of time it takes to say something or to respond. For example, in a Robert Wilson dialogue, an action-reaction cycle can take five seconds ("Are you leaving?" "Yes") or hours, depending on how the action unfolds and is answered. It is by awakening our ability to hear this flow of action and reaction in its full range that we hope to create truths on stage, *within* various aesthetics in response to the specific "nows" of performance.

---

3   The support for this assertion is discussed in full in my PhD thesis: *VOCAL ACTION: From Training Towards Performance.*

> Truth is a tricky word and an even trickier concept. In the twenty-first century, there is no such thing as 'objective truth' any more: your perspective is as legitimate as my perspective which is as legitimate as anyone else's perspective. Each person's vision of the world is to be as justified as anyone else's. Which is fine, because when it comes to TRUTH, what we're really looking for is a *context* for what we're seeing, some rules which determine our expectations, some kind of LOGIC AND COHERENCE [...] the key to this sense of TRUTH is the ongoing sequence of Action–Reaction. [italicized emphasis added] (Merlin 114)

Regarding the structure of the day, I always begin with intensive psychophysical exercises. This is a kind of "back door" approach. Instead of focusing on a specific skill such as "resonance" and developing it through a repeated exercise that centers on the mechanics of that work, the students engage in more flowing physical structures in which various requirements for "resonance" are provoked, such as open and free ribs, a flexible and responsive diaphragm, or released but listening muscles. In this context, the student experiences re-finding the resonance that their body "naturally" has, than a sensation of "working on" resonance. Practically, I structure my exercises around exploring action-reaction cycles in different materials (sound, text, song) sparked by a wide range of impulses: imaginative, physical, spatial and sonic. This approach is based on a common underlying assumption held by many voice practitioners: that the body *knows* how to use itself correctly, and when there is a clear need, the unconscious body-voice's deep knowledge will respond appropriately, counteracting any learned "block" of the conscious body. After these embodied experiences, we move on to technical exercises, specifically ones that explore more "conscious" techniques of rediscovering physical positions within the voice. These exercises arrive from a school of thought that views the body as a machine, and which suggests our "free" and "natural" voices have been crippled by the bad habits of modern living, and so promotes a healthy readjustment. Teaching exercises based on two common but oppositional ideas and allowing them to exist beside each other brings them into dialogue, without giving either a privileged position. These exercises form the first half of a two-part session, which I refer to as *vocal presence*.

Historically, there was a one-to-one relationship between training and performance forms: both had the same aesthetics and thus there was little difficulty for performers transitioning from training to performance. This is no longer the case. Today students sometimes leave school with a bag full of tools, but no understanding of how to employ them in the new aesthetic forms they meet. I would argue that it is very important that in *each* training session, there is a dramaturgical movement from training towards performance. In the second half of my training sessions I focus on *vocal composition*, or the application of these "essential exercises" within the confines of a specific aesthetic. The range of application I use is wide, from improvised sound installations in the dark, to songs of tradition, to working on Shakespeare monologues. I draw on strategies from Devised methods, as well as older compositional techniques. Often I work simultaneously on contrasting aesthetics, so that students can have the experience of applying the same principles within two different performance forms. In each of these applications, it is also of course necessary to employ some aesthetic-specific techniques. For example, when working with Shakespeare, I draw on the work of Cicely Berry, seminal voice coach of the Royal Shakespeare Company, whose rich work offers much to the young performer. In composition work, I always historically contextualize the method, allowing the students to first explore "what has been done" before they embark on their own exploration of "what has yet to be expressed."

> In the twenty-first century we have the entire panoply of methods and sounds available to us […] Today we have a chance […] to be in charge of how our music is to be created, how we communicate it to other people. We can experience the liberating value of being at the origin of our creative acts. (Nachmanovitch "On Teaching Improvisation")

Like the Sankofa bird of West African mythology, it is paradoxically because we must look backwards that we can walk forwards. I propose here not a revolution, but a few small shifts in how we as teachers contextualize and think about our own work, and how we as students look to simultaneously respect and question what we are given. From this new perspective, we teacher/students can assist in creating performers who can contribute to a long living tradition of aural knowledge passed down through voice work, as well as reinvigorate live performance by bringing to it new voices that speak of the holistic-fragmented, chaotically ordered realities that we live in today.

References

Barba, Eugenio and Nicola Savarese, eds. *A Dictionary Guide to Theatre Anthropology: The Secret Art of the Performer*. London: Routledge, 2005 [1991]. Print.

Gordon, Robert. *The Purpose of Playing: Modern Acting Theories in Perspective*. Ann Arbor: University of Michigan Press, 2006. Print.

Govan, Emma, Helen Nicholson, and Katie Normington. *Making a Performance: Devising Histories and Contemporary Practices*. London: Routledge, 2007. Print.

Martin, Jacqueline. *Voice in Modern Theatre*. London: Routledge, 1991. Print.

McAllister-Viel, Tara. "(Re)considering the Role of Breath in Training Actors' Voices: Insights from Dahnjeon Breathing and the Phenomena of Breath." *Theatre Topics* 19.2 (2009): 165-180. Print.

McAllister-Viel, Tara. "Voicing Culture: Training Korean Actors' Voices through the Namdaemun Market Projects." *Modern Drama* 52.4 (2009): 426-448. Print.

Merlin, Bella. *The Complete Stanislavsky Toolkit*. London: Nick Hern Books, 2007. Print.

Nachmanovitch, Stephen. "On Teaching Improvisation: A Talk with College and University Conductors." Freeplay.com [accessed November 21, 2011].

Oddey, Alison. *Devising Theatre: A Practical and Theoretical Handbook*. London: Routledge, 1996. Print.

Zarrilli, Phillip, ed. *Acting (Re)considered: A Theoretical and Practical Guide*. London: Routledge, 2002. Print.

Scenography and the Visual at Norwegian Theatre Academy

Karen Kipphoff

The Norwegian Theatre Academy is a place of artistic learning and experimentation by production. Throughout the twenty years of its existence, this truly tiny school of less than thirty students has developed into an intensive acting and scenography laboratory. The Academy's particular environment is partly shaped by its location on the outskirts of a small, almost rural city, removed from the capital but situated in a historically and culturally rich landscape: a mix of early and post-industrial buildings, farmsteads, and villages in soft, rolling hills. Water is also a strong visual factor: the omnipresent North Sea and the rivers embrace Fredrikstad. This semi-urban land- and seascape sets the milieu for the small group of Norwegian and international students, artists, and organizers who meet and work at the Academy. Here, students collaborate in student-led (as well as directed) independent productions and workshops. Ingredients for these artistic works are readily developed, prepared, "cooked," and presented for each other and the audience under the auspices of distinguished artists and experts from overlapping fields of the stage and other arts, including visual, sound, media, architecture, urban, and landscape art. Scenography is here understood as the development of spatial contexts and the creation of situations that visualize shifts within artistic productions over time. The pedagogical approach to scenography at the Academy can be summarized as the teaching of embodied experiences of visual, audible, tactile, and sometimes olfactory aspects of the artistic process. This allows students to answer to, interact with, compliment, comment upon, counteract, and juxtapose artistic expressions, while flooding a space with a fluidity of form, color, texture, and spatial insertions. In a learning process, big and small things need to be placed and moved physically around the stage in order to really understand the materiality of objects, subjects, space, and time. Only then are we able to respond with the creation of the appropriate visual and light settings for a performance. The aim of the NTA is to create shifts in perception, which in turn open new doors to other contexts and perspectives on the potentiality of scenography in the widest sense of the word, including stage design, exhibition design, and art in the public space.

Responsive Listening

Photos

Everything Ends with Flowers, 2012. Directors: Juli Apponen and Jon Skulberg. Photo by Monika Sobczak.

Wash your hands until they get holes, 2009. Director: Andrey Bartenev. Photo by Ioannis Lelakis.

Daily Life Everlasting, 2014. Written by Charles Mee, directed by Dan Safer. Photo by Jan Hajdelak Husták.

Enjoy the Silence, Dancing Queen, 2013. Director: Dan Safer. Photo by Monika Sobczak.

Sculpture, 2013. Independent Production by Marie Kaada Hovden. Photo by Marie Kaada Hovden.

Taking Turns, a walk through performance for one spectator, 2013. Independent Production. Director: Paolo Zuccotti. Photo by Jan Hajdelak Husták.

Music, Weather, Politics, 2014. Homlungen Lighthouse at Skjærhalden/ Hvaler; workshop as part of Prague Quadriennale/Shared Spaces. Photo by Serge von Arx.

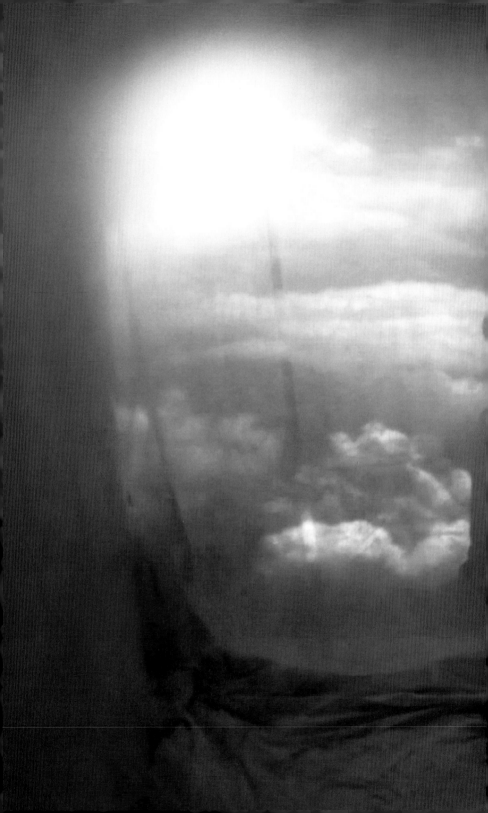

Text as Sound and Music

Øystein Elle

To what extent might an aural, abstract treatment change the perception of textual material? What can musical adaptations of linguistic sounds add to the understanding and experience of text? In this brief article I want to elucidate some aspects of text in performance by comparing text and music and discussing how texts have been, or can be, interpreted sonically in performance.

I am a singing performer—not just a singer, if anyone ever is. That is, I am someone who responds to the signs that other people produce—sounds, written words, images, gestures—by changing them and re-creating them in new contexts, as part of a long tradition of experimentation with the production of meaning through performance.

I often detach letters and words from their lingual and narrative function, seeing them as building blocks with individual qualities. I utilize both of these approaches, along with game structures, in my textual reconstructions, thus bringing a linguistic *chance* element into the work that may or may not add elements of meaning.

We tend to seek meaning in a text. Whether the text is conveyed in a performance setting, or read from a book, we may think we are being presented something that is "true" to the original. But what if the original were simply a starting point for all kinds of ways of responding, ways that radically change the original, add to it, clarify it, or make it more meaningful? If we assume that the text is what is written down, then the sonic treatment has an executive function. After having retrieved information from the written characters, this information is reinterpreted, and then sent out as sounding-language. The sounding-language may be consistent with what the characters represent, phonetically; at other times, the practitioner might perform a linguistic translation of these characters adjusted so as to reach a certain type of receiver. These adjustments could serve different purposes: for example, let's say the performer believes that the receiver of the text does not understand the written language, or perhaps the recipient is a child. In this case, the performer of the text might want to adjust the textual content, or simplify it, in order to make it more easily comprehensible. Or one might move in a different direction, treating a text as a source of a more sonic, less narrative experience. In either case, it is the job of performers of text characters to communicate and/or interpret.

When performing notated music, I relate most often to scores with some form of notation. Music compositions are usually presented to a musician as notation signs to be interpreted and conveyed by the performer. Sometimes the composer has imagined a sounding outcome from the musicians' interpretation of the written signs; other times, the musicians are freer in their shaping of the sounding result. How it is communicated is dependent on many factors, such as the skill of a musician, a musician's sense of style, geographical origin, cultural origin, curiosity, creativity, obedience, habit, or tradition. Text is also often presented as abstract signs that must be exerted by some force or individual in order to be transformed into lingual sounds, which the author might assume represents relatively indisputable language sounds, but which is not always the case. One may ask, then: does the music exist before it is performed? Or, does the text exist before it is interpreted? If so, in what form?

Text can be as abstract as notated music. The concretization of a text is a way to give it a language. This may be close to the author's intention; maybe one even receives instructions from the author. Alternatively, as a performer, you are more or less free to interpret and convey any textual material the way you wish. I do not necessarily see aural treatments of texts as a process of abstraction; I may as well see it as a concretization of abstract characters. Often the method used to communicate various written texts relates to the expected aesthetics of a certain context related to place, time (era), genre, etc. What changes the perception of the textual material is *how* the sonic treatment is carried out.

The German multimedia artist Kurt Schwitters wrote his sound poem "Ursonate (Sonata in Primal Sounds)" between 1922 and 1932 (see Figure 1). Its form is similar to a classical sonata or symphony, and consists of four movements: *Prima parte*, *Largo*, *Scherzo*, and *Presto*.

Schwitters said about his writing: "The elements of poetry are letters, syllables, words, sentences. Poetry arises from the playing off of these elements against each other. Meaning is only essential if it is to be used as one such factor. I play off sense against nonsense. I prefer nonsense, but that is a purely personal matter. I pity nonsense, because until now it has been so neglected in the making of art, and that's why I love it" (Kolocotroni 282).

Ludwig Josef Johann Wittgenstein claimed that language is a prerequisite for consciousness. Further, he said that language sets the limits of our consciousness,

Responsive Listening

INTRODUCCION:

Fümms bö wö tää zää Uu,
    pögiff,
        kwii Ee.
	1

Oooooooooooooooooooooo,	**6**

dll rrrr beeeee bö
    dll rrrrr beeeee bö fümms bö   (A)
        rrrrr beeeee bö fümms bö wö tää,
            beeeee bö fümms bö wö tää zää,
                bö fümms bö wö tää zää,
                    fümms bö wö tää zää Uu:
	5

PRIMERA PARTE:

Tema 1:	Fümms bö wö tää zää Uu,
	    pögiff,
	        kwii Ee.
		1

Tema 2:	Dedesnn nn rrrr,
	    li Ee,
	        mpiff tillff too,
	            tillll,
	                Juu kaa?
		2

Tema 3:	Rinnzekete bee bee nnz krr müü? ziiuu ennze, ziiuu rinnzkrrmüü,	**3**
	rakete bee bee,	**3a**
Tema 4:	Rrummpff tillff toooo?	**4**

EXPOSICION:

Ziiuu ennze ziiuu nnzkrrmüü, Ziiuu ennze ziiuu rinzkrrmüü, Rakete bee bee? Rakete bee zee.	**ü3**
rakete bee bee? rakete bee zee,	**ü3a**

Figure 1

our universe. If that's the case, then within the sounds of language lie our futures, our hopes. If language sets the limits of our consciousness, where do we end up if the language sounds are not maintained or developed?

In my own work as a researcher and performer, I am often searching within the text to discover and identify something beyond its narrative function. I listen to what the text gives me, what it says, beyond its linguistic function. To do this, one might consult radio programs in foreign languages, not to learn the languages, but to enjoy timbres, rhythms, and musical structures undisturbed by meaning. One can release more content from a text by treating it first as a source of sonic experience. Perhaps by taking the text's musical, instrumental, and aural qualities and possibilities seriously, one might even add important values to a narrative structure.

As a tribute to my favorite word, I wrote a poem:

AFAL

Ja moma mas
Pom Macel
Po m me mas
Po ja Eplka m pppplko mapel
Jas
Polm
Pomapple
Jablmome anza mukape
a pla mablma a Ma melkomanana
elë ma Ma Mabumo
mo a masa
el mo elale
muko pl Eppelë
Ma Mabuko Mas
Jana
mafanaple
Jaceira pelelle

Responsive Listening

It is a construction of the Norwegian word *eple* (apple). First, I translated the word through fourteen languages. Then I treated these fourteen versions of the word through a text generator, which is based on a probability calculation, aptly named the Markov Chain, by the Russian mathematician Andrey Markov. Online generators and other machines, digital or analog, can be very helpful when reworking existing text. The important question is, if the words are rearranged, is it still the original text? What if the letters are rearranged? Will traces of the author's consciousness survive the transformation? Can this "new language" provide another way of understanding text, on a level other than the purely cognitive?

More on this idea of sound poems: I find it interesting to borrow linguistic sounds and gather vocal data concerning vocal aesthetics from around the world and have them act congruously as a nomadic voice travelling through time and space, working with traces from the past—harmonically, melodically, linguistically. It would also be interesting to chart how sense and non-sense differ according to the approach of a listener, within this context. Nonsense literature is a solid branch of literature, a broad and diverse genre, which includes children's rhymes and jingles that offer many directions of interpretation, challenging linguistic conventions and logic. Here are two sentences I found connected to nonsense, chosen to illuminate the divergent views on the genre:

> Nonsense literature is effective because of the human desire to find meaning everywhere, in everything, and where perhaps none exists.
> —Jean-Jacques Lecercle

Text as Sound and Music

The effect of nonsense is often caused by an
excess of meaning, rather than a lack of it.
　　−Wim Tigges

When working with a text, I often come to a point where
I wonder whether the meaning of the text has disappeared
from the experiment (the experiment being either with your
own text or with a work of existing material).

But getting back to the idea of text scores as a form
of musical notation: some leave a great deal of freedom to
the interpreter; others are more strict and precise in their
instructions. Here is a notation for "Stones" by Christian
Wolff:

Make sounds with stones, draw sounds out of
stones, using a number of sizes and kinds (and
colors); for the most part discreetly; sometimes in
rapid sequences. For the most part striking stones
with stones, but also stones on other surfaces
(inside the open head of a drum, for instance)
or other than struck (bowed, for instance, or
amplified). Do not break anything. (Nyman 114)

Another example of an instructing text score is "Wind
Horse," by the American composer and performer Pauline
Oliveros (see Figure 2).

In both scores, the textual material is a prerequisite
for the sounding artwork. With the first, a common
understanding of the written language is necessary for
the outcome; in the second, the map, the pattern, spatial
associations, and the written words all work together to
guide the performer toward an individual interpretation

Responsive Listening

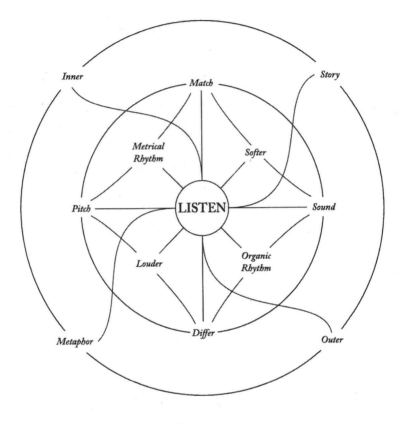

Figure 2

sprung from listening and presence. The main point is that both texts are open to interpretation, however the performer sees fit. And if we as performers un-ground our voices from conventions connected to textual deliverance, we can enjoy infinite possibilities for textual interpretation and seek a reception from the audience that goes far beyond the usual cognitive limitations.

Text as Sound and Music

References

Kolocotroni, Vassiliki, Jane Goldman, and Olga Taxidou, eds. *Modernism: An Anthology of Sources & Documents*. Chicago: University of Chicago Press, 1999. 282. Print.

Lecercle, Jean-Jacques. *Philosophy of Nonsense: The Intuitions of Victorian Nonsense Literature*. London: Routledge, 1994. Print.

Nyman, Michael. *Experimental Music: Cage and beyond*. London: Macmillan, 1999. Print.

Tigges, Wim. *An Anatomy of Literary Nonsense*. Amsterdam: Rodopi, 1988. Print.

Notes

"Wind Horse" image used with the permission of Pauline Oliveros. "Wind Horse" created by Pauline Oliveros with additional design by Lawton Hall.

The example from Kurt Schwitters' "Ur-Sonata" detailed in Figure 1 is but a representative piece, being the first page of a longer work.

Zooming In:
Reflections on My Education
at Norwegian Theatre Academy

Veronika Bökelmann

The first task of my acting audition at the Norwegian Theatre Academy (NTA) in April of 2004 was to create a three-minute performance on one of two themes: "Zooming In" or "Sink or Swim." While most European acting programs asked applicants to prepare two to three monologues for male or female roles according to the applicant's gender, NTA allowed applicants to audition according to their own artistic interests and background. I prepared a documentary-style dance-based piece, *Augustine*, which "zoomed in" on the psyche of a hysterical patient in the Parisian clinic Salpêtrière in the 1880s. The audition's task made clear the Academy's distinctive artistic imperatives: exploration of theater forms that are not a *necessary* subordinate of dramatic texts, and an active investigation of proximities between art disciplines, from theory to social practice. These were the qualities I had been looking for in my theater training.

When I first arrived at Fredrikstad's train station from Berlin, with its mere two-rail tracks, I realized how much "zooming in" my education would require in this low-speed, small town, where there was not much else to do than focus on my studies. In my view, a lot of the intensity and creative friction the Academy generates is derived from the dichotomy of being rather geographically secluded, on the one hand, and yet, due to its outstanding educational and artistic profile, being very well connected to both a local and an international contemporary theater network. The questions I would like to answer here are: where does this sense of connectivity come from? How does the Academy remain unique and vibrant? And which aspects have I taken further into my professional life?

Acting Beyond Representation

Apart from the skill training and some other fixed modules, the structure of our education at NTA was predominantly workshop-based, in order to give insight into different traditions of thinking and making theater. For the acting students, this meant that the development of characters and the representation of dramatic roles were understood as only *one* of many methods of acting and performing. When my class first gathered in August 2004, I could see how a declined importance of representation within acting had also softened a few fixed categories and norms established in classical theater training regarding gender, race, and age. My class was made up of nine students from six different countries—seven women and two men, aged 18-25 years. I was the oldest in my class, and already seen as "too old" for "classical" acting training. Unlike many other programs, NTA's jury members prioritized the personal qualifications of its applicants over the need for a "truthful" representation on stage. For instance, my outstandingly talented classmate Huy Le Vo, who is Norwegian with a Vietnamese ethnicity, might have had a harder time getting accepted at a "classical" acting program, as specific racial features could impede him from exploring representative "neutral" roles (in a tradition of psychological-realism) within the predominantly white

Norway. As a consequence, the colourful mixture of my classmates directly countered existing societal power structures by embodying critical theories.

Intensity and Fluctuation

The entire Academy, both the acting and the scenography departments, consisted of only twenty-six students. Together, with international guest teachers and the staff members, we formed a small, vibrant, English speaking "interzone," in constant fluctuation and redefinition.[1] The guest teachers seemed to like to visit NTA, both because they could experiment with the students as young co-artists, and because the small-town environment allowed them to slow down from their busy lives in New York, Brussels, Berlin. This produced an intense connection, a closeness, between guest teachers and the students, which I had not experienced during my tenure at the University of Arts in Berlin nor later at New York University. In a way, studying at NTA felt like an extended artist residency: we shared a luxurious, well-equipped space with the teachers, who gave us generous insights into their methods, and who guided and advised us in our own artistic explorations. Those personal relations can enhance one's professional networking skills and often lead to long-lasting connections—for example, Andrey Bartenev invited several NTA students to participate at the Moscow Biennale for Young Artists in 2008, and I personally was invited by Six Viewpoints founder, Mary Overlie to study with her in New York as an exchange student during my last year at NTA.

---

1   William S. Burroughs coined the term "interzone" in his novel of the same title to refer to the then vibrant "International Zone" of Tangier in Morocco.

Optionality, Depth, and Emancipation

A key element of our education was to make our own choices in terms of what we, individually, wanted to explore further in depth. What kind of actor/performer/artist did we want to become? Where did we want to set our focal points? What did theater mean to *us*? The modules of "independent productions" and "laboratories" gave us official space and time to experiment with solo or collaborative creations, which we utilized at night. Some of my co-students practiced singing after class, performed acrobatics, or investigated character work. In the evenings I created video-body-space installations and successfully sent out applications to media art festivals in Canada, Oslo, Serbia and Montenegro. In this sense, our education certainly demanded a high amount of self-responsibility, which resonated for me as "intellectual emancipation," in Jacques Rancière's understanding of it, rather than neoliberal terms. An emancipation because the training at NTA does not solely endorse or teach a given set of methods, it prompts aspiring actors and scenographers to redefine theater on their own terms, and provides the tools to help explore its different manifestations. In the most positive way, then, the teachers at NTA function as "ignorant school masters": they "teach what [they] do not know" (teaching that they *cannot* give one definition of theater). By doing so, they proclaim "the happy message of intellectual emancipation,"[2] and invite students to discover for themselves what theater can be: "What do you see? What do you think about this? What will you do with this?"[3]

---

2   Rancière, Jacques, *Der Unwissende Lehrmeister* (*The Ignorant School Master*). Vienna: Passagen Verlag, 2009. (My translation from the German.)

3   Ibid, pg 35.

Modes of Collaboration and Theater Forms

Determining which forms of theater to participate in or to create for our selves was very closely connected with experimentation and collaboration. The well-curated educational models were divided into two types of laboratories: directed and independent productions. Even within the directed productions we experienced many different modes of organizing social and decision-making processes due to the variety of guest artists "directing" us, such as the Volksbühne Berlin actor-director Milan Peschel, or the Norwegian performance group Baktruppen, which is famous for its flat, non-hierarchical structures. Each mode of collaboration shaped the aesthetic and relational outcome of our performances to the extreme.

Most importantly, though, was how much our work was influenced by the close collaboration between actors and scenographers. From our very first workshop in August 2004, a two-week laboratory for both scenography and acting students,[4] not only did we share courses but we also collaborated in the creation of performances, where acting students were trained in developing an awareness of space, both physically and conceptually, and the scenography students learned to create theater from the point of view of the body. In my understanding, the close collaboration between the two departments has generated many genuinely extraordinary theater and performance works, often coined by the equivalency of body and space. The absence of directing students in positive terms forced us to find alternative, often non-hierarchical ways of working

---

4   Our first workshop, entitled "Learning about Seeing," was an introduction to the composition of basic elements of theater, such as space, body, movement, text, social relation, and objects.

and thinking about theater; this is perhaps similar to the applied theater-science education in Giessen, where the non-presence of acting students might have stimulated aspiring artists like Stefan Kaegi (Rimini Protokoll) to work with "daily life experts" instead of with actors.

After School

For me personally, the collaboration with scenography student Séverine Urwyler at NTA directly resulted in the realization of my first professional production in 2008: *Tyskerjenter* (War Brides). The documentary theater installation was set on Hovedøya Island, where Norwegian war brides were interned after WWII.[5] The performance is thematically linked to my entrance examination piece for NTA on hysteria: both works deal with the pathologization of female sexuality and desire. In many ways, *Tyskerjenter* directly reflects the artistic development I underwent at NTA. For the entrance piece, I used a chair with twisted limbs to represent a hysterical patient—pretty straightforward; in the walk-through performance of *Tyskerjenter*, Séverine and I created a much more complex, affective architectural and relational space, a space in which the performers' and audience members' bodies, the historical site, and archived texts all interacted and resonated with each other. Norwegian theater critic Therese Bjørneboe, wrote of the piece in *Norsk Shakespeare-og Teatertidsskrift* that the performance pointed to possibilities of documentary theater beyond

---

5   *Tyskerjenter* was kindly supported by Norsk Kulturråd, Goethe Institut, Fond for Lyd og Bilde, FFUK and Fritt Ord. More about the performance on: www.volumenexpress.com and http://www.youtube.com/watch?v=9mK2KX8tF40.

the "staging of amateur-actors" a la Rimini Protokoll.[6] She added that the piece "tears down dogmas of how to deal with authenticity in contemporary theater,"[7] and, in my opinion, it does so as a result of our education at NTA, with its intimate training of scenography and performing practices.

De-/Professionalization

We were able to realize a production of such grand scale shortly after graduation because during our education we were trained to work as performing artists professionally on the open market: we had courses in budget and production planning, application writing, and in documentation of artistic works.[8] In many ways, both Séverine and I left the Academy with a feeling of empowerment; we trusted our practical skills to realize complex projects and our artistic experience to critically engage with societal issues. We felt professionally reassured when approaching potential funders, venues, and collaborators. We had the disciplinary openness to step into varied working fields—such as conducting historical research in archives—and we had the theoretical knowledge to critically place our works in an art-historical context, and to talk and write about it in public. Seven years after graduation, many of those aspects still feed my professional life. NTA's vibrant "interzone" had prepared me to navigate the transnational field of theater and performance art with relative ease, and I have kept creating

---

6   Bjørneboe, Therese. "Teatertidsskrift." *Norsk Shakespeare-og* Jan. 2009:95.

7   Ibid.

8   The application of *Tyskerjenter* to Norsk Kulturråd directly resulted from a seminar on application writing with Pea Hov.

performances at diverse places such as Buenos Aires, Halden, and Berlin. NTA's multidisciplinary approach has enabled me to work in-between fixed categories, oscillating between installation, performance, and multimedia art. Furthermore, it has allowed me to switch naturally between professional roles, which have included curatorial projects for film programs and work as a theater critic.

Yet, having realized several big, efficient "projects," I wonder if NTA has perhaps educated me *too* well to act within the short-term rhythms dictated by a cultural funding system predicated on predominantly neoliberal values. Today I almost wonder how I can de-professionalize myself from the thoroughgoing rationalization and efficiency that I have incorporated, as larger questions have now become pressing in my professional life. If we, as transnationally operating performing artists, embody many of the values of the neoliberal "virtuoso"[9,10]—such as short-term thinking, creativity, flexibility, "projectification," willingness to (self)-exploit, remain constantly mobile, engage in competition, etc.—how can we produce art works and collaborative structures that do not just reproduce the current mode of production and subjectivity? How can art educational systems continue to reflect and embody alternative, critical values, and, yet, still produce artists who are "successful" in the current political economy? It

---

9   Compare with Paolo Virno's *A Grammar of the Multitude*, Semiotext(e), 2004. For Virno, virtuosity in Post-Fordism coincides with the qualities of the "performing artist."

10   Compare further to Luc Boltanski's "The Present Left and the Longing for Revolution." *Under Pressure: Pictures, Subjects, and the New Spirit of Capitalism.* Eds. Birnbaum, Daniel and Isabelle Graw. Berlin: Sternberg Press, 2008. Boltanski claims that capitalism has incorporated the "artistic criticism manifested mostly through demands for self-management...that is, through demands for employee control of firms' management, and for enhanced personal autonomy and creativity."

is the responsibility of teachers and performers, both, to open spaces in order to share our experiences of failure, precariousness, and the performance of resistance.

A Good Thing:
A Graduate's Tale

Ivar Furre Aam

It was a misty summer morning on the outskirts of the central Oslo. I was drinking coffee with my good friend Sorin Aleksejevitsch Verbukov Finnevavov, the younger, on our veranda, overlooking a small garden. Some birds were singing, as if they wanted to get it over with, before the heat of the day got the better of us. The sun shone through the branches of a large birch. I had gone to bed early the previous night, but for Sorin, who seldom knew what was best for himself—which was one of the traits I most appreciated about him, his ability to get into trouble due to a complete lack of self-preservative instincts—it had been a long hard night dedicated to drinking and loud discussions with the theater intelligentsia. I, on the other hand, always took precautions. I would make sure to get to bed early.

Sorin had come home to our shared flat just as I got up to have a glass of water, after having spent the night tossing and turning, battling my inner doubts about theater and the influence it has in the world, the result of a passionate love for an art form I often dislike. We decided to share a large bottle of beer and continue our discussion from last evening on the nature of theater. What was revealed I will never forget.

"You see," I said to him, "when I perform a play, I feel perhaps contradictory—more honest when I quote the words of a playwright, someone who is not me, than when I speak as myself. Sometimes when I read the lines of a character, I get the feeling that this is just how I feel."

"That is very interesting indeed, Pjotr Nikolai Lvov," Sorin said, "but why does this matter?"

"It matters because the actor should always take a conscious position towards what he is playing."

"Yes, but why does it matter if you are honest or not? In what way does that make anything better, and how does that contribute to new experiences for the audience. And yourself?"

I was a bit puzzled by his sharp response.

Having noticed that I was taken aback, he continued, "I'm sorry, I didn't mean to bark at you. I'm just not in a very good place these days. I'm having a hard time defining what it is that I am doing...with my life, with my art, yes, everything actually."

"Tell me about it. I feel this way on a regular basis, in fact, right now I am working on an essay entitled *On Doubt*, where my main theory is that doubt can be more productive than both motivation and enthusiasm, so maybe I can help?"

"Thanks. You see, I make the performances I would like to see myself," Sorin said. "The problem is, as I see more and more, and learn more and more about art discourse, methods, techniques, and if my ideology is, let's say...to create the possibility of experiences of the new, I'm in deep shit, because the more I know, the new will be harder and harder to produce. Perspective, knowing, or at least relating to what has and is happening in one's field is obligatory in other systems of knowledge production—law, fine arts, dance, football, literature—but a large part of the theater field seem completely oblivious to this. Believe me. I spent tonight with a bunch of them and all they do is compare head

A Good Thing

shots, and it literally made me feel like getting shot in the head. But, could this be an advantage? Because producing the possibilities of the production of new experiences with the awareness of what is going on is hard work and demands a nitty gritty, hands-on, let's-just-put-this-thing-together-and-analyze-it-later attitude. Or an enormous capacity for self-deception. Not confidence, which is the basis of capitalism. And certainly not enthusiasm. Sometimes I wish I could just erase everything I know and become an amateur again."

Sorin stared off blankly, reminding me of one of Warhol's video portraits. I imagined he was picturing his new career as a mindless theater director.

It sounded true what he was saying. I did not agree with him, since I was more interested in working with *difference*, in the Deleuzian sense, but Sorin was in a strange mood and I did not want to discourage him, so I just nodded and said, "That sounds interesting, but did you not say that gaining knowledge about your field is a good thing?"

"That might very well be so. I am not sure what I am getting at, but let me just tell you about my background, I know you know me well, but sometimes I find it easier to philosophize when I just let my mouth run."

"Of course," I said, and wrapped my woolen blanket closer around me, as the morning was still chilly.

"Well," Sorin shifted in his chair, "I started at the Norwegian Theatre Academy in Fredrikstad in the fall of 2006. I was twenty years at the time. After three years I had obtained a bachelor's degree in acting. Since then I have been working as an actor, director, dancer, dramaturge, in the institutions, outside of the institutions, in Norway and outside of Norway, with contemporary theater, classical theater, contemporary dance, and conceptual choreography. I did an MA at Stockholm Academy of Dramatic Arts, which was about artists who make their own work. You know very well that I draw a sharp line between my work as performer, in the works of other artists, and my own work, although the positions merge and influence each other. So, let me first give you a short account of how I work as a director, since that is mainly where my problem lies...what I have drawn from my years in Fredrikstad, and how I perceive the NTA now. But first I will take you trough a series of detours."

Sorin took a pack of cigarettes from his pocket and put one of the cigarettes in his mouth, patted his pockets looking for a lighter, paused, and started talking again.

"It's been five years since I left the protective environment of the fortified old town of Fredrikstad with two questions: was the old town protecting us from the world, or were the walls and moats in fact protecting the world from us? And, what do I do now? I was 23 at the time. Should I worry?"

"Yes," I was trying to sound helpful. "Don't worry. I mean. Worry, yes, yes! You have a BA in acting, you're basically fucked, but, you know, not too much. Prepare for the worst and hope for the best. Or so they say, anyway, where were you?"

Sorin found his lighter, light the cigarette and started smoking it greedily.

"The week after I graduated, I received a phone call. The guy on the phone offered me a job, in a real theater. Ironically, after spending three years explaining to ignorant theater workers that I was not actually acquiring a puppeteering education, that I *really* hated puppet theater, my debut in a "real theater" turned out to be as the main character in a puppet musical. I was a flat fish in a triangle drama involving a crab and a swordfish. Reality hits you smack in the face with its fin. Despite the prolongation of my solitude—Molde was not grossly populated, but neither was Fredrikstad—I enjoyed it tremendously. We performed the play seventy five times. The same year I also began performing a monologue for teenagers, sometimes twice a day, before lunch. I performed that monologue over eighty times. After three years of going over continuous variations of methods and short projects, it felt great to repeat one piece many times over, even if it was in front of a bunch of hormonal teenagers with a set design that changed every day. Go do Den Kulturelle Skolesekken, my dear Pjotr, to experience what a real audience is like.

"After that year, I went on to the Stockholm Academy of Dramatic Arts, which was headed by a Belgian actor whom I had already worked with in Fredrikstad. The MA had a name, The Autonomous Actor. The program was similar to Fredrikstad in how it combined theory and practice, introducing us to various contemporary artists. The people in my class were so autonomous that after the program we all drifted our own different ways, occasionally coming together to perform, mostly naked in French immersive choreography. I know it might come as a surprise, but I have only performed naked in two works.

"The MA program added to the confidence I first experienced in Fredrikstad, especially since the participants in the program came from more traditional theater schools. They'd worked in various institutions and came to the program for a different approach, where I, on the other hand, saw the education as a prolongation of what I had been doing all along in Fredrikstad. We also spent time with the MA people studying choreography, and, in spite of their occasional pretentious display of art discourse—you know, being pretentious is the only way of really getting anything done, but you have to stop it before the audience enters—we felt we had more in common with their projects than the theaters of Sweden, which aren't as interesting as the institutions in Norway, but are often more engaged politically. In Norway, there is a growing understanding of formal expansions into the territory of the new, but what we want to talk about with our art, and what positions theater makers in Norway take, is not much problematized. We're all just trying to get into movies...I think it has to do with geography. But also that the potential of theater is not fully realized, as in *making people conscious of*, here. In Sweden, *political* is something you want to be, or have to be, in order to be taken serious at all; in Norway, it's more like "it would be nice to do something a little political," but not too much, because then no-one will take you seriously."

Sorin was getting more and more into it, his mind was racing, and I had to do my best not to interject and let him have his say.

"Fredrikstad is an interesting little exception, but it is also the source of my problem. Before I go more into what I have been doing professionally, and how that has been informed by my years behind the walls, I need to explain how I regard the education in Fredrikstad. Are you familiar with rhizomatic learning, Nikolai?"

I had to admit, that no, I was not.

"The usual way of mapping knowledge or education is as some sort of tree. We start with the stem and reach out into branches and twigs and leaves. An arboreal image. You are familiar with Deleuze, the French philosopher, died in the 90's, I think? Yeah? He came up with the rhizomatic depiction of knowledge. In a tree map of knowledge, you have to learn something before you can learn another thing, and as you reach branches of the tree, certain things are not connected anymore. The rhizome mapping, which I think is a better way of viewing how knowledge was circulated in Fredrikstad, is flat and connected in various ways. It allows for connections between seemingly unconnected things, like butoh, or method acting—working with how mental images affect the body, for example. If you look at what each student retains, like an old moldy wool blanket, it will be thicker in some places and thinner other places, depending on that student's personal interest. Thus some students, or generations of students, might have a strong movement base, where others were stronger vocally or conceptually. The way the education is curated makes the experience of the different generations of students quite varied—we did not have the same teachers, we did not have the same heads of departments, and so on and on, but this rhizome structure of our knowledge allows for us to move cross-generationally, intertextually, between fields."

"So it is more like an academy where you pick and choose?" I asked.

"No," Sorin responded, annoyed, "it's not about shopping an education, because the students can't really choose for themselves in real time, only afterwards. This is one of those similarities repeated through generations of students who labor under hard self-scrutiny for three years in this lovely little place: we don't know the same techniques, or hold the same viewpoints, or realize whatever is hot at the moment, but we all adhere to this structure of knowledge with more or less success. We all know that there is definitely no "One

Truth"—here Sorin did his Ian McKellen impersonation for emphasis—"with regard to theater or acting, because once a teacher asks us to perceive a thing one way, the next teacher will contradict the first one. And so on and so on. It is a very unorthodox, non-authoritarian pedagogy, or so it seems."

"Yes," I said, "you could wonder then, if authority becomes something else in this situation, like say, The New, or originality, the demand for creative solutions, or saying that you must always like what you are doing. It reminds me of Žižek explaining morality in totalitarianism with the story of a father who yells at his young child: "You must come and visit your grandmother!", leaving no doubt about what is to happen. There he claims authority. On another occasion, though, he quietly explains to his child: "You know how much your grandmother loves you, but you should only visit her if you really want to." As both we and the child understand, there is actually two commands in play on the second occasion: not only must you come and visit your grandmother, but you must also like it."

Sorin paused for a moment, and touched his forehead lightly, as if thinking hard. "Yes, you might be on to something, but it is beside the point. Well, because, other acting schools in Norway are more arborous, in that they are based on a system of knowledge founded on one master practitioner, such as Stanislavski or Lecoq, and one has to ask: what do these structures produce in the student? In Bergen they did an interesting survey on medicine students and psychology students. The psychology program in Bergen is structured similarly to NTA, in the way that the students learn about a whole range of different methods, not specializing in one single method. The students from both schools were asked after the first year how much they felt they knew. The medicine students on average answered that they felt they did not know much, whereas the psychology students responded that they felt they knew a lot. After six years, they reproduced the survey, but this time this picture had turned around completely. Whereas the medical students now answered that they knew a great deal, the psychology students felt they knew very little."

"How can this change over six years?" I asked. "Certainly the psychology students in their final year know a lot more than in their first year."

"The cause may be that the psychology students do not know less, but that they know more about what they do not know."

"Do you think this is symptomatic of the difference between specialization and acquiring broad knowledge?" I asked.

"It might be," Sorin said. "It might just be so, but the real question is, what do you do with the knowledge of knowing you know less than you know?"

"In the 80s, the French philosopher Jacques Rancière published a book called *The Ignorant Schoolmaster* about a seventeenth century French teacher named Joseph Jacotot. Jacotot one day found himself schooling parents on how to teach their children to read; the thing was, the parents did not know how to read themselves. But it worked, they taught themselves to read. So a parent learns to read along with his child, teaching a subject about something he knows nothing about. The main point of this argument is that in a traditional master/pupil relationship, there is a double authoritarian power play: not only does the teacher understand the knowledge the pupil does not know, she also knows how it is that the pupil does not know. The pupil is thus both ignorant in regards to the knowledge and she is ignorant about her own ignorance. Rancière, in the essay "The Emancipated Spectator," which was really popular in 2008, but now I feel it is a bit passé, and certainly not contemporary, goes on to argue that this relation of power is also valid when describing the situation of the performer and the audience. The ignorant schoolmaster's position is therefore a more emancipatory position, since the pupil gains knowledge of his own ignorance when forced to prove his ability to learn what is not being taught.

"In Fredrikstad this is repeated. Let's say, for the sake of the argument, that you think of the institution of NTA as a teacher. Since there is no overarching "master" study, such as Stanislavski technique, but rather curated contemporary artists who arrive as project-based teachers, the school becomes, in a sense, ignorant of what it is teaching. It contradicts itself as an academic institution and produces a third position between the cracks of what is being produced. As an institution, it sources knowledge through different persons and is therefore itself ignorant of the production of knowledge that is conveyed to the students. The student is therefore forced, in a sense, to access his own ignorance, and though they have guides, these project-based teachers, who do not adhere to a standard curriculum and teach separately what they wish, the students are largely responsible for their own education. This is interesting because, as NTA hopes to educate contemporary actors, it is impossible to tell what kind of actors will be produced, or will be needed in the future contemporaneity.

"At the same time as it creates uncertainty, because you lack specific coordinates as a student, and because your need for confirmation is challenged and the confirmation you receive from one teacher might well be dismissed by the next, I loved the very concrete measurable skill training I received there, precisely because it was measurable. And I could see that I was getting better at connecting the various trainings I received. But that took tough, rigorous reflection, which can make whining cowards of us all."

"So what do you do with the knowledge of you own ignorance?"

"It seems to me that you have several options. You can specialize in what you dig. You can use analogy: I know something about contact improvisation, how can I use that to produce dramatic text? Or you can use your ignorance to create a work as I did with my latest piece, *The Expressions of the Emotions*. In it I investigate on stage the production and labor of emotions, deconstructing one of the main means an actor possesses to activate his craft, whether fake or real, and reconstructing it for a mise-en-scène that balances between abstraction, ambiguous reality, and a production of fiction. It is a composition of expressions, without a narrative, but occasionally relational. One of the reasons I wanted to examine this theme was that I felt that I was bad at expressing some of the emotions onstage.

"Another thing I learned in Fredrikstad was that you must construct your own method or borrow one that conceptually suits the thing you want your play to do. With *The Expressions of the Emotions* I took something I knew about, choreography and composition of movements, and used the technique of method acting to expand them. Actors on stage try to instill within themselves certain emotional states while remaining true to the choreography of their expressions. Sometimes they fail, sometimes they succeed. A great deal of the tension in a play is produced by the possibility of failing; the payoff is what the audience gets when actors succeed. But of course this would never be possible if the actors were accomplished method actors. Amateurishness makes for a harder, truer form of realism."

"But, then," I said carefully, "you don't seem to have a problem..."

Sorin became silent. "Yes...perhaps you are right. Thank you for listening. I don't think I would have been able to come to that conclusion on my own. On that note, I still have something I very much would like to discuss with you. How I work as a theater director and an actor/performer in other artists' work differ. I have mostly explained how I think as a director, that the method you choose for producing your work naturally affects your work..."

I got up from my chair and quietly went inside. Sorin raised his voice for me, but was so into his own thinking that he hardly cared that I had slipped away into the kitchen to make coffee and begin working on my notes.

"You know, the easiest way of de-territorializing your production and produce new things is to change the modes of production."

I decided not to drink coffee but chose instead to go back to bed and see if I could catch some more sleep before rehearsals. As I lay down I could still hear him talking to himself on the veranda.

"A performance made in a kitchen will look different from a performance made in a blackbox. Some would say that various works are not at all exhibiting the process that lies behind the result. I say no, because it is a part of the process of their creation, to hide it. It is always visible, always, if you know what to look for. What Fredrikstad handed me was a way of consciously choosing a method that produces what you want, instead of being stuck with a method that diminishes your options. And that is a good thing..."

Contributors

Ivar Furre Aam is an artist and director in the fields of contemporary dance, theater, and transdisciplinary performance art, producing work with his company either on his own initiative or in collaboration with other artists. Ivar makes work that deconstructs theater and investigates the media specific potentialities of theater and performance while challenging notions of production of emotions and individualistic tendencies in western culture. In addition, he works as an actor and performer in theater, film, and dance with other artists companies and choreographers such as the Norwegian National Theater, Sidney Leoni, Lisa Lie, and Trøndelag Theater. He is currently an artistic consultant at the Norwegian Actors' Center. He holds a BA in Acting from Norwegian Theatre Academy/Østfold University College and an MA from Stockholm Academy of Dramatic Arts.

Electa Behrens is associate professor of voice at Norwegian Theatre Academy/Østfold University College. She holds a Practice as Research PhD from Kent University (UK). She has performed with many companies and artists throughout Europe and the USA, including Transit Teatret (NO), Odin Teatret (DK), Richard Schechner (USA), Marina Abramovic (Serbia), Dah Theatre (Serbia), F2 Performance Project (Greece) and the Centre for Performance Research (Wales). As researcher and practitioner, she has participated in Paul Allain's British Grotowski Network and Britain/Russia, an exchange with the Moscow Arts Theatre School, as well as participating in three *Giving Voice* festivals, organized by the CPR.

Born 1978 in Germany, **Veronika Boekelmann** is currently based in Berlin and works as artistic assistant at the department of Fine Arts/Architecture at Technical University Berlin. Veronika holds a MA in Performance Studies from New York University and a BA in Acting from Norwegian Theater Academy/Østfold University College. She previously studied at the Institute for time-based Media at the University for Arts in Berlin (UdK). As founding member of the artist collective VOLUMEN EXPRESS and friends, her art work explores the borderline of installation and performance, often engaging with the relation of the archive, the body, and (urban) environment. She realized large scale performance installations such as *(Im)Potencia* (Sophiensaele Berlin, 2010; Black Box Theater, Oslo, 2010; Club Cultural Matienzo, Buenos Aires, 2011), the site specific work *Tyskerjenter—War Brides* (Island Hovedøya, Oslo, Norway, 2008/09), and the audio video walk *Present Past* (Oslo, 2013). Further, her prize winning video installations have been shown at festivals like Video Medeja Festival (Serbia and Montenegro), Film Winter Festival (Stuttgart), or Moscow Biennale. In 2012-13, Veronika held a scholarship from the DAAD—German Cultural Exchange Service, and in 2009, she received a one-year working grant from the Norwegian Cultural Council. She has also worked as external curator for the Norwegian Film Institute, as guest lecturer at KhIO, NTA, and at the film academy in Ludwigsburg.

Camilla Eeg-Tverbakk is currently a research fellow at Norwegian Theatre Academy, and PhD student at Roehampton University, London. From 2007 to 2011, she held the position of Artistic Director for the acting program at Østfold University College/Norwegian Theatre Academy.

She works as dramaturg in independent projects as well as in collaboration with directors and choreographers in Norway and internationally. She has also been active as a curator, teacher, and lecturer since 1997. She trained as performer and theater artist at École Jacques Lecoq, and holds an MA in Performance Studies from NYU, and an MA in Theatre Science from the University in Oslo. Eeg-Tverbakk was the editor of *Dans i samtiden*, a book on Norwegian contemporary dance (Spartacus 2006), and *Performance Art by Baktruppen, first part* (Kontur 2009).

Øystein Elle is currently employed as an artistic research fellow at the Norwegian Theatre Academy/Østfold University College. Previously he was an assistant professor at the same institution, teaching voice, singing, and improvisation/composition. He studied singing (baritone and countertenor) composition, conducting, and piano at the Music Academy in Utrecht, the Netherlands (MA), and at the Conservatory of Music at Agder University (BA). He works in several disciplines as a performing and creating artist: singer, actor, composer, and producer, as well as having developed his own interdisciplinary artistic projects. As a singer, Øystein specializes in the field of Baroque music, but with his experience in various bands, and as a performer of contemporary and experimental music, he often mixes various musical expressions. As a performer and as a composer, Øystein has worked at a number of theater institutions and independent groups, including Dansens Hus, Theatre of Cruelty, Teater Innlandet, Nord Trøndelag Teater, Dramatikkens hus, Karstein Solli productions, Østfold Teater, and was a co-founder of the Oslo Baroque Opera. As composer, as solo performer in various music ensembles, and through his multi-year collaboration with Karstein Solli Productions, Øystein has visited festivals and toured Norway, Germany, Finland, Israel, Chile, Brazil, Italy, France, and the Netherlands. He has also premiered a number of musical works by foreign and Norwegian composers.

Karmenlara Ely is the current Artistic Director of Acting at Østfold University College/Norwegian Theatre Academy. Before coming to Norway, Karmenlara taught at New York University's Tisch School of the Arts, where she holds a PhD in Performance Studies. She collaborates as a performer, dramaturg, and scenic costumer on theater, festival, and performance works in New York, Northern Europe, and the Americas, including recent projects with Spiderwoman Theater. She is the project leader for the Norwegian artistic research project *Infinite Record: Archive, Memory, Performance*, with institutional partners at Massachusetts Institute of Technology in the US, York St. John in the UK, and Muthesius Kunsthochschule in Kiel, Germany. Karmenlara teaches performance workshops and lectures internationally. Her research focuses on the critical roles of the body and desire in taboo breaking performances and on the complexities of pleasure and consumption in artistic processes.

Karen Kipphoff was educated as a visual artist, puppeteer, and in drama education in Germany. Kipphoff has worked at Schaubühne Berlin, Kammerspiele Hamburg and Theater am Turm, Frankfurt. She uses photography, performance, and installation as her artistic medium and has exhibited and performed at the Museum of Contemporary Art Bucharest, Bergen Kunsthall; The Museum of Novyj Sad, BIT

Teatergarasjen Bergen; and at Uferstudios Berlin. Previously she taught in Bergen and Berlin and is presently a professor at Østfold University College/Norwegian Theatre Academy. In 2011 Karen Kipphoff co-founded the Performance Art Bergen network, organizing and co-curating several events. Recent publications include *Never? Now? Performance Art!, Horizon* (Revolver Publishing Berlin, 2012), and *Instrumental Objects as Playful Subjects* (Oslo, 2014).

Serge von Arx, Professor of Scenography, is the Artistic Director of the Scenography Department of Norwegian Theatre Academy/Østfold University College and an independent architect and scenographer. In 1997 Serge von Arx earned his degree in architecture at the ETH Zurich (Swiss Federal Institute of Technology). After two years of work experience within architecture and exhibition design in Paris, he began his professional career as assistant stage-designer in Hamburg. In 1998 he began collaborating with Robert Wilson on numerous stage, exhibition, and installation design projects all over the world. Since 2003, he has been a regular mentor and architectural consultant at the "Watermill Center" on Long Island, New York. In 1999 he became a member of the Swiss Association of Engineers and Architects. In 2001 he opened a design studio in Berlin and since 2006—the same year he was appointed the Artistic Director of the Scenography Department at Norwegian Theatre Academy—he has been a resident of Oslo. Serge von Arx expanded the academy's portfolio with a MA in scenography, launched in early 2015. Today he lectures and implements workshops at various international universities and other institutions. Serge von Arx's research focuses on the encounter of architecture and theater. He inquires this field of "performative architecture" in theory with various international publications and in practice. Currently Mr. von Arx is curating the architecture section for the Prague Quadrennial 2015.

Acknowledgments

We want to first of all thank our diverse students and alumni who have influenced the development and research of our approaches to acting and scenography. We also wish to thank all the teaching, technical, and administrative staff who make this education possible on a daily basis. Finally, we want to thank the influential guest artists and pedagogues who have visited and taught at Norwegian Theatre Academy, and who inspire and challenge our approach. This includes our artistic council: Robert Wilson, Meg Stuart, and Kelly Copper and Pavol Liška of Nature Theater of Oklahoma.

We want to extend our gratitude especially to Østfold University College, for its support in the development of this unique theater education since its origin.